Che
mar/21

Lisa Wo... ...n away for
generatio... ...grandfather
was a du... ...all her life,
and in recent years has taken photographs of her beach and river finds.
She is the author of two award-winning photography books about the
sea, and *Rag and Bone* won a Royal Society of Literature Giles St Aubyn
Award for Non-Fiction. She has lived in Cornwall with her family
since 2004, in a house shared with buckets and boxes of shore finds.

'Lisa Woollett's beautifully descriptive language intertwines the stories
of the river's history with that of her family, like a muddy journey
through time. But it's so much more than that – in recording the
waste and the lives we've left behind she's given us a chance to change
our ways and possibly head towards a cleaner future'
RAYNOR WINN, author of *The Salt Path*

'Absorbing . . . Woollett has a gift for bringing to life the strange
borderlands of the foreshore'   *Observer*

'Lisa Woollett spins narrative gold out of literal dross in this gorgeous
story of our waterways'   *Evening Standard*

'Discursive, lyrical and intriguing . . . Woollett writes beautifully'
Literary Review

'Wonderful . . . If you loved *The Salt Path*, you'll love this book. A
glorious celebration of where the natural world meets the human
(and the messes we make)'   VIV GROSKOP

'*Rag and Bone* digs deep into the mud of the Thames estuary, and
comes up with something compelling and urgent . . . Lisa Woollett
is a genuine mudlark, alert and closely attuned to the ways of the
intertidal zone. A fascinating book'   PHILIP MARSDEN

'Subtle, dark and funny, with flashes of beauty and wonder, *Rag and
Bone* is a compelling meditation on consumer culture and its consequences'   CASPAR HENDERSON

'More than personal memoir, this is a powerful book that has much
to say about the present and future state of our world'   *Countryfile*

'A constant delight'   *Eden Magazine*

Also by Lisa Woollett

Sea and Shore Cornwall:
Common and Curious Findings
Sea Journal

FOR CHILDREN

Treasure From the Sea

Rag and Bone

A History of
What We've Thrown Away

LISA WOOLLETT

JOHN MURRAY

First published in Great Britain in 2020 by John Murray (Publishers)
An Hachette UK company

This paperback edition published in 2021

1

Maps drawn by Tracy Watts

A CIP catalogue record for this title is
available from the British Library

Paperback ISBN 978-1-473-66398-5
eBook ISBN 978-1-473-66397-8

Typeset in Bembo MT by Palimpsest Book Production Limited,
Falkirk, Stirlingshire

Printed and bound in Great Britain by Clays Ltd, Elcograf S.p.A.

John Murray policy is to use papers that are natural, renewable
and recyclable products and made from wood grown in sustainable
forests. The logging and manufacturing processes are expected to
conform to the environmental regulations of the country of origin.

John Murray (Publishers)
Carmelite House
50 Victoria Embankment
London EC4Y 0DZ

www.johnmurraypress.co.uk

For the Tolladays

Contents

Note on Safety

Anyone wishing to search the tidal Thames foreshore must hold a current foreshore permit from the Port of London Authority. They also provide details of potential hazards and dangers, recommended safety precautions, reporting requirements and restricted areas. When mudlarking or beachcombing anywhere, always be aware of tide times and exit points to avoid being cut off.

Introduction: Lansallos, Cornwall

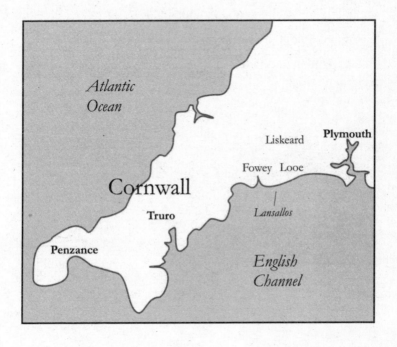

Atlantic
Ocean

Liskeard

Plymouth

Fowey Looe

Cornwall

Lansallos

Truro

Penzance

English
Channel

I paused from poking through seaweed, straightening up to disentangle the wiry tendrils of a mermaid's purse. It was the egg case of a nursehound shark, thrown up during overnight gales, and as it was empty I dropped it in a deep coat pocket. Out in the bay the sea was still wild and uneasy, and for a while I watched gulls sweep along the troughs ahead of waves, before lifting off into sunlit spray. Otherwise the beach was deserted and I returned to my methodical search among the heaps of weed, picking through dulse, oarweed and sugar kelp. On shore they had lost their lazy, waterborne elegance and the glistening reds and ambers had the look of magnificent costumes tossed aside.

Having grown up by the sea on the Isle of Sheppey, at the mouth of the Thames, I'd been searching beaches since childhood. I started out collecting old bottles, and sifting the shingle below our house for fossils and sharks' teeth. Then, as now, I also searched the strandline left at high tide, keeping a razor shell, perhaps, or the dark, horned egg case of a ray – clues to unfamiliar and hidden worlds offshore. All these years later, beachcombing still feels like hunting for treasure, although now I'm just as likely to keep the man-made flotsam, for its often telling reflection of ourselves.

At home, the finds I keep tend to accumulate first in various halfway houses, drying out on ledges and windowsills. As I write now, those lined up at the edge of the nearby bookshelf include a sponge and several barnacles, a plastic leaf and the lid from a Smarties tube, a whelk and something I suspect is the melted end of a roll-on deodorant. In the darker recesses of the shelf above, other finds can sit forgotten for years, gradually making their way further back into the crowded disorder of fossils, shells and dusty jars.

Back in my twenties I lived in London and worked as a photographer, but I moved to Cornwall when our son was a year old. Here, unable to work in the ways I had before, I began photographing the sea and selling prints through galleries – initially preferring stormy, elemental days, in part as an antidote to spending so much time with babies. It was then that my childhood beachcombing resumed in earnest. As many of my Cornish finds were a mystery, I began researching them and was soon finding any excuse to take the children to the beach, gripping hands at the edges of cliffs to take one-handed photographs, and rubbing bloodless white fingers back to life as they emerged from the sea. We searched together and brought finds home to look them up online and in books, their sharp eyes finding things I would otherwise have missed. We stayed in the van or with friends at the coast – and once at a youth hostel, remembered as the one where my son hid the dead triggerfish under the car bonnet so as not to have it in our room (writing FISH in the bonnet's dust to remind us not to drive off with it still there in the morning). By then the children were taking finds into school for show-and-tell, and their friends would save me bags of washed-up bones.

Now my daughter is eleven. She is still a keen beachcomber and in the right mood can be doggedly persistent and competitive (when very small she would refuse to keep fossils if she suspected they'd been 'planted'). She is also shrewd, watching my reaction closely to see what a find might be worth as a swap. So she keeps her collections separate to mine and has some great finds hidden beneath her bed. Yet this year is her last at primary school, so that may be about to change. At fourteen, her brother comes with us less often. His rock collection was passed on several years ago and he has little attachment to the things he finds, either leaving them behind or handing them straight to us. Several times recently, I've caught myself wondering if something will soon have slipped away. At home is a cabinet of finds from those early years and I've felt it becoming increasingly precious. Behind the glass is an old print setter's tray from the local car-boot sale, filled with flat-bottomed test tubes. Inside each is something we found on one of those childhood beach trips: a few cowries, a teddy's eye, an inch of sand, the jawbones of a sea urchin, a small plastic boat. Some of the tubes also have a slip of paper curled inside the glass. On most I wrote a date and the name of the beach, and on the reverse something that happened that day. Yet in the years since, I've never opened them to see what I wrote. The tubes are sealed with a cork and through the glass I can read little or nothing of the biro scrawl. Instead, I imagine opening them when the children are grown. Perhaps they'll describe things I've remembered anyway. Or might they be things that would otherwise be lost?

These days my local beach is in South Cornwall. It's a good half-mile walk down a wooded valley and, as always, much of the attraction lies in having no idea what I will find when I get there. In the quieter summer months this might be no more than a few crab moults or translucent scraps of weed. Yet at other times gales and heavy seas can bring huge changes overnight, and I've sometimes arrived to find tonnes of sand dragged offshore or banked against cliffs. Often, as today, there are heaps of stranded weed, along with the usual assortment of broken and wave-worn flotsam – I'd already passed a split bucket and a boot, several plastic bottles and the remains of a fishing crate. I've been visiting this beach regularly for well over a decade now and frequently check the forecasts, yet any expectations I have can still be spectacularly wrong.

Just occasionally I've emerged from the passage in the rock to find something extraordinary. Once it was hundreds of Portuguese men o' war, littering the grey sand like gently deflating balloons, in impossibly exotic electric blues and pinks. Another time it was glittering whitebait, and on several occasions the intricate skeletons of by-the-wind sailors – a distant relative of jellyfish – their stiff sails scattered along the strandline and blown up against cliffs. Mostly, though, it's been similar to today, with heaps of weed and plastic fairly typical for this beach after gales. Yet there could just as easily have been nothing at all, as more than once I've returned the next day to a beach that was littered with debris to find the night's high tide has swept everything away, taking back all its clues, its treasures and its indictments.

I stopped for a wet bundle of rags and fishing line. I'd learned from a friend to check these for the remains of pink sea fans and today, as usual, found several in the tangle. They are a type of horny coral that in life are beautifully sculptural colonies of animals, although their skeletal remains look more like polished twigs. Extremely slow-growing and vulnerable to trawling and dredging, they have been on the Red List of threatened species for decades. Once broken off, their dense woody skeletons sink to the seafloor. Drawn along by the currents, any sunken rags and detritus can then snag on their branches, gathering in bundles that sweep along the seabed. I've seen all sorts caught up in these, from zips and strings of beads to fishing lures, sunglasses and pants elastic. I teased this one apart to see what else it might contain, but as it was just cloth and fishing line I dropped it in the rubbish bag I'd brought along – which as usual seemed a token gesture, as there was so much else I'd leave behind.

Amongst the weed I spotted the remains of yet another plastic bottle. This was just the flayed neck, worn in a particular way that is common on this stretch of coast. I've lived nearby for almost a decade and a half now and it took a while to get to know the new beach: to adjust to its seasonal and tidal rhythms, to new species, to the way it wore its plastic bottles. Usually, the parts I find are those that last longest: the thicker necks and bases. Without a lid to trap air, the clear polyethylene doesn't float, so as usual this one had been scoured by the waves and sand, perhaps thrown ashore and washed back out repeatedly. I picked it up. I already had a number of similar necks and bases at home, worn into clear geometric shapes that remind me of plankton – perhaps appropriately, given that the plastic is made from oil, which in turn was made from plankton over millions of years. While I had no need for yet another flayed bottleneck, I slipped it in my pocket with the mermaid's purse.

A month earlier, in that same cove I'd found what I thought at first was the body of a gull. It had washed up on a bed of wrack and was strikingly pale against the dark of the weed, with the creamy feathers of its underside uppermost. I only realized it was a fulmar once I was close enough to see the beak. Exquisitely curved at the tip, it was as pale as the bird itself, with the distinctive feature of its curious 'tubenose'.

In Britain the fulmar is the closest we have to the legendary albatross. Both species belong to the same family – the tubenoses or 'order of the storm birds' – with its members ranging from the least storm petrel to the magnificent wandering albatross. Like the other storm birds, fulmars spend almost their entire lives at sea; as well as enhancing their sense of smell, their tubenoses – raised tube-like structures on the top of the beak – are used to excrete excess salt from drinking seawater. The word fulmar is from the Old Norse and means 'foul gull', a reference to the birds' habit of spitting a foul-smelling oil as a form of defence. Due to the vast distances fulmars travel at sea, they are unable to bring back whole fish to feed their young, so the oil also preserves energy-rich nutrients in the folds of their stomach, which can then be regurgitated when they reach their nest. Unlike most seabirds, this leaves them with only a very limited ability to regurgitate indigestible parts of their prey, such as bones or squid beaks – and likewise any debris eaten by mistake. As fulmars feed only at sea, for decades scientists have been recording their stomach contents as an indicator of trends in ocean plastic pollution.

Afterwards, I watched several short films showing dissections of fulmars found washed up on North Sea beaches. At white laboratory benches the birds' small stomachs were placed in glass dishes, bulging at odd angles until the taut membranes were pierced with needle-nosed scissors. One was packed with hard-edged plastic fragments, another entirely blocked with pieces of plastic sheeting that were carefully unravelled to record their full size. From the stomach of one bird, the researcher extracted a bag of silica gel – the kind packaged with new electronics – and read the words still legible on the side: 'Gel. Do not eat. Throw away'. A number of white-coated scientists had gathered to watch the dissection and there was a ripple of ironic comment and hollow laughter.

In carrying back these snapshots of the debris drifting at sea, fulmars are described as a 'sentinel species'. Research shows that 95 per cent of fulmars from the North Sea now have plastic in their stomachs, and it is estimated that by 2050 this will be true of 99 per cent of all seabirds. By then – only a century after this revolutionary material began entering our homes – it is also predicted that by weight there will be more plastic than fish in the sea. Watching dissections of tiny, distended fulmar stomachs, it is hard not to wonder how we could possibly have got to this point.

At home, my favourite finds are behind glass in the kitchen cupboard. Where at first these were mainly natural, over the years more man-made finds have been creeping in. So alongside the sea urchins, the anglerfish jawbone and razorbill skull are now two Lego dragons and a rusty steel toecap, half a sea-worn cassette tape, a naked-looking table-football man and a white plastic gull. Another favourite is the wizened kelp with its holdfast still attached to a golf ball.

As well as beach finds, the lower shelf now holds river finds too, collected on mudlarking trips to the Thames. For the past few years I've been visiting the foreshore at low tide whenever possible – which, as I live in Cornwall, isn't as often as I'd like. Mudlarking is possible on the Thames because it's tidal right up through central London, each low tide revealing part of the riverbed for several hours at a time. While mudlarking has many similarities to beachcombing, it is also very different – not least because the anaerobic Thames mud is such a wonderful preserver. So the finds in the kitchen cupboard now include the rims of two Roman cooking pots, some medieval pottery, various clay pipes, a musket ball and a seventeenth- or eighteenth-century bone comb. The comb had fared particularly well in the mud and, as was common at the time, has a fine-toothed side to tease out nits. Beside it leans its modern equivalent: a wave-worn plastic comb missing most of its teeth.

Prompted by this growing collection of discarded shore finds, now spanning many centuries, I've kept returning to a branch of my family that included dustmen and a scavenger. Their surname was Tolladay – my mum's maiden name – although beyond my grandad's generation I'd known almost nothing about them. But I was keen to find out more, so recently I'd traced them back over several more generations and found that in 1841 they lived at Water Street beside the Thames in central London. I already knew that over subsequent generations they'd moved downriver to the estuary and, eventually, the sea. So for someone keen to spend as much time as possible searching beaches and the foreshore, this suggested an irresistible route, with potential sites ranging from creek shores littered with London's barged-out Victorian rubbish to beaches close to my childhood home, where 1980s fly-tipping erodes from the foot of the cliffs.

PART I

The Thames

I

Wapping to the South Bank

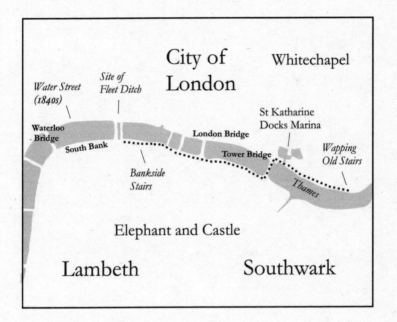

Although I'd traced the Tolladays back in the records, I wasn't sure how much more I'd be able to find out. For while everyone in the family spoke warmly of my dustman grandad, no one seemed keen to talk about his dad. Until I'd begun following that backwards trail through the censuses – poring over yellowed ledger pages beneath the gloss of a computer screen – my family had no idea where the Tolladays came from. And the more I thought about it, the more I realized that although I'd heard plenty of family stories over the years, almost all of them came from my nan's side.

All I'd seen of that earlier generation was a single black-and-white photograph, taken a century ago at a wedding in Southwark. I'd been shown it only once as a teenager and remember little more than that they were an odd mix of very short and very tall. Yet even that picture no longer exists, because some years later, as my nan's memory began to fail in her eighties, she started to cut people out of photographs. These were often members of my grandad's family and, when I asked later about the photograph of the wedding, I was told she'd cut that one to pieces.

Some months after finding the fulmar, I set out for the first walk to Water Street. Along the way, before catching up with the Tolladays, I wanted to consider some of London's pre-Victorian history. I'd chosen to start at Wapping, partly for a family connection, but mostly because it was once at the heart of London's maritime trade. From there my intention was to walk the few miles to Water Street upriver along the Thames, crossing over to the south bank for the middle stretch and walking on the foreshore wherever I could. From the day's chance finds – lost, dumped or discarded – and those I'd picked up along this stretch before, I hoped to piece together an impression of the city as it grew up around the river. At Wapping, in particular, I wanted to look at the changes that came through the Early Modern period, from the fifteenth to the eighteenth century, as global trade and colonization linked England to distant parts of the world, before that great turning point of the Industrial Revolution.

Now, having crossed London on the Tube wearing wellies (which always gets a few glances), I walked into Wapping through cavernous streets overshadowed by luxury warehouse conversions. When I reached the alley leading through to Wapping Old Stairs it was sunk in shadow, slicing between buildings to a strip of sunlit shore. It was on this narrow stretch of higher ground that Wapping's early settlers made their homes, hemmed in by the river on one side and low-lying marsh on the other. From medieval times they were protected from floods by river walls made of earth, with records showing them destroyed in 1323 by 'vehement tempests from the sea'. Yet they were subsequently rebuilt and in time the settlement became Wapping-in-the-Wose (the Middle English *wose* – later ooze – meaning mud or mire).

While the Romans had chosen twin gravel hills for the site of Londinium, the land to the south and east of the city remained part of the floodplain. There, a much wider, shallower Thames formed the main channel of a braided system of tributaries and streams, which wound their way through marshes and swamp. Core sediment samples taken from beneath London's streets show there were also a number of shifting river islands or eyots, which live on in the odd borough name. Bermondsey, for example, was once 'Beormund's Eyot' – thought to have belonged to a Saxon Earl Beormund – and similarly Hackney may also have been 'Haca's Eyot'. So while the city of London grew steadily as a centre of medieval trade and commerce, the poorer ground to the south and east was much slower to develop.

As elsewhere, London's rivers were its earliest dustbins, so amongst the historic fragments littering the foreshore it's not uncommon to find traces of the medieval city. So far my own medieval finds had mainly been pottery, made from a coarser clay than the smooth Roman pot rims and flecked with 'inclusions': fine pieces of shell, flint or quartz added to the clay to prevent pots cracking or exploding in early kilns. Several fragments also had a mottled green glaze – the first coloured glaze used in Britain – which from the eleventh century was produced in potteries along the Thames waterfront. My favourite was the handle of a late medieval 'Surrey whiteware' jug, its thick clay scored with distinctive slash and stab marks, which again prevented breakage under the stress of early firing.

At the time, London's overcrowded homes meant much of life was lived out on the streets, which were noisy, raucous and often dangerous. They were also filthy, as the city found it increasingly difficult to cope with the waste generated by its growing population. A great deal of refuse and household waste was simply thrown or emptied out into the streets, often into a central gutter or 'kennel' that drained water away from the houses. From the twelfth century, London's streets were in such a state that people began wearing pattens – wooden or metal over-shoes that raised the wearer above the fetid mire.

With the city's streets becoming close to impassable, the job of clearing the muck and rubbish fell to 'rakers' and later 'scavagers': the very beginnings of London's organized refuse collection. The waste they gathered would be carted away and either dumped in the river or transferred to what were known as 'gong boats'. *Gong* is from the Old English *gang*, meaning 'to go', and described both a toilet and its contents – which constituted a major part of medieval waste. Known as 'houses of easement', a number of London's early public toilets were situated at the edge of the Thames, so the contents would be sluiced twice a day by the tide (one fifteenth-century 'house' is recorded as having two rows of sixty-four seats, with one row for women and the other for men). Others – often little more than a plank with a hole – were sited on bridges over the Thames and its tributaries.

As well as a source of water and power, London's rivers were also where much of its industrial waste was dumped. Gradually, as the old riverside fishing trades were pushed out, they were replaced by more polluting industries. In central London some of the earliest were the potteries and cloth dyers, with their spent dyebaths emptied straight into the Thames. At the time, bleaching involved vats of sour milk and cow dung, and binding agents such as the ammonia in stale urine. One particular shade of medieval green required, among other things, the dung of a dog and a dove. Other colours included Puke (a dirty brown) and Sad (a dark shade of any colour), with the range extended later to include Rat's Colour, Horseflesh and Gooseturd, along with the pale greyish-tan Dead Spaniard.

As London grew, much of its polluting industry continued to be sited along its riverbanks, from tile kilns and breweries to slaughterhouses, mills and tanneries. These waterways included tributaries of the Thames known today as 'lost' rivers, as most now run underground through sewers. Being smaller than the Thames, they were more quickly overwhelmed by pollution. Most notorious of all was the Fleet, which in the thirteenth century was deep enough to allow a trade route from the Thames up to Holborn. At the time two monasteries stood on its banks, with their White Friars and Black Friars – named for the colour of their hooded robes – already petitioning the king in 1290 about the river's 'putrid exhalations'. These 'overcame even the frankincense', they wrote, 'and had caused the death of manie Brethren'.

One grim source of the Fleet's pollution was Smithfield, Britain's oldest meat market, sited on the river's east bank and producing a steady stream of waste carcasses, blood and offal. By the fourteenth century, following repeated outbreaks of bubonic plague, Smithfield's butchers were instructed to dump their waste in the Fleet to keep it off the streets. (Another of the butchers' routes, the famous Pudding Lane, takes its name from the piles of entrails – 'puddings' – that slipped from their carts on the way to the Thames.) In time the Fleet's lower reaches were little more than a vast open sewer known as Fleet Ditch. The valley became synonymous with poverty and squalor, and tracts of its cheap, undesirable land were bought up to build prisons; by the sixteenth century these included Newgate, Bridewell and the Fleet debtors' prison. Clogged with refuse and waste, and with industry diverting its water to mills, the Fleet became increasingly impassable for ships, so periodically it needed to be dredged. On at least one occasion, the silt dug from its riverbed contained refuse dating back to Roman and Saxon times – arrowheads, daggers, crucifixes, a statuette of Bacchus – showing that the Fleet, like the Thames itself, had been London's dustbin from the very beginning.

At Wapping Old Stairs, the gloom of the alley opened out at stone steps leading down to the shore. Like other watermen's stairs on the Thames, they are close to a pub, the Town of Ramsgate (until 1766 it was called the Red Cow, allegedly after the colour of the barmaid's hair). I made my way carefully down granite steps green with weed, each stone both foot-worn and river-worn.

Halfway down a man in waders stood pouring coffee from a flask. We nodded hello and from the gear strung about his body – a spade and metal detector, laden rucksack and metal sieve – I presumed he was a mudlark (although some are detectorists, most use no more than a trowel and would describe their technique as 'eyes only'). Feeling a little underprepared with my carrier bag, bottle of hand sanitizer and emergency butter knife in lieu of a trowel, I made my way out towards the water's edge. I trod over wet pebbles and river-bottom rubble, old roof tiles, broken pottery and shingle to the fine Thames mud.

There was no one else on the shore and no passing boats. The river was like silk, undisturbed by wake as the ebb tide withdrew from the city and slipped back out to sea. That morning in particular, it was hard to imagine the clamour that would have surrounded these stairs in the past. As well as the loading and unloading of goods, vast numbers of watermen plied their trade, clustering around the steps with shouts of 'oars!' and 'sculls!' From the sixteenth century, the number of watermen's stairs had increased steadily as more and more of the Thames was walled in. Many considered the river safer than the city's narrow, crowded and often dangerous streets, and the stairs functioned as taxi ranks: designated safe places, where the watermen could pick up and set down their passengers.

It wasn't far off low tide. I stooped along the water's edge, crouching when I reached a patch that was crowded with nails. Still wet from the tide, in the early sunlight they were rust oranges, reds and blue-greys. There are similar patches all along the foreshore – the tide sorting its trash and its treasure by density – and over weeks or months they might barely move. Then one day, perhaps on a spring tide with strong winds or heavy rain, everything can change. When the river draws back the metal is gone, laid out and rearranged elsewhere, like the last sweep of a magician's hand.

I pored over the metal, not scraping or digging but just looking: a slow, methodical sweep to and fro as I waited for something to stand out. Often what caught my eye was some kind of regularity: an edge, perhaps, or a pattern, a curve or circle, a colour like the grey of lead. That day, though, it was mostly nails. Some would be relics from the sixteenth and seventeenth centuries, when ships were built this close to the city, before they grew in size and shipbuilding moved downstream. The oldest nails were square-shanked and tapered, some beautifully preserved by the mud. I chose a couple, then another. I had more than enough at home but can't always help myself, swayed by colour, by the way one has bent, by the precise edge of a beaten shank. Hand-forged by a blacksmith, each would have been laboriously hammered into shape on an anvil and then reheated to attach the head. This was a time-consuming process, changing little from Roman times to the Industrial Revolution, and meant that nails were valuable enough to be salvaged and reused.

I straightened up from rinsing mud off what turned out to be no more than a modern washer. The river was barely moving. With no visible flow either up or downstream, I guessed it was close to slack water. The well-equipped mudlark was nowhere to be seen. A few feet away, I caught sight of a crescent of pale clay sitting just proud of the mud: the edge of a pipe bowl. I pushed my fingers in, twisted fractionally to see if there was give. There wasn't, which was good. It meant there was more beneath the surface. Held close by the mud, the pipe was entombed where centuries ago it had come to rest, perhaps thrown from a wharf or ship. I wiggled it, but the river was unwilling to give it up. I twisted further and could see that the bowl was unbroken. But how much of the delicate stem? I eased it slowly, carefully from the mud. Of all the various pleasures of mudlarking, this was perhaps the most satisfying.

At last the pipe slipped free of the undermud, not whole but with a decent length of stem.

I was pleased to have found it where I did, as the family connection to Wapping was that Tom Tolladay – my scavenger great-grandfather – married into a family of clay pipe makers originally from Bluegate Fields. Long gone now, this pretty-sounding place turned out to be a notorious slum behind Tobacco Dock, built on the drained marsh around Wapping-in-the-Wose. By the late nineteenth century Bluegate Fields had become synonymous with crime and debauchery, and featured in Oscar Wilde's 1890 novel *The Picture of Dorian Gray*, its brothels and opium dens the scene of Dorian's corruption and moral decay.

I rinsed the pipe and wrapped it, keen not to immediately break something that had lain safely in the mud for centuries. Although pipes are common finds along much of the foreshore, particularly fragments of stem, it still felt good to find one. The satisfaction was partly aesthetic – the clay has a fine, chalky surface – but also because a pipe is such a tangible link with the past. From the shape of the bowl, this one was eighteenth century and it was likely that no one had touched it in 300 years, since someone took a last puff and threw it in the river (perhaps because the stem had clogged with tar). This was quite possibly a dockworker or sailor, and it was also common for them to intentionally break the long stems, either to remove blocked ends or to allow smokers to work with both hands free. One study of skeletal remains from a cemetery in nearby Whitechapel found that many of the skulls had notches worn in the front teeth, where they'd habitually held a clay pipe. A few had an almost perfectly circular hole.

By the eighteenth century, when my pipe was discarded, this stretch of river was the busiest in the world. London was now the gateway to an empire and, as a rapidly expanding merchant hub, saw goods pouring in from across the world – from India, the Caribbean, Africa, China – both for the British market and transfer overseas. As well as thousands of watermen, every kind of craft imaginable was on the water, from fishing smacks, dung boats and coal barges to Arctic whalers and merchant sailing ships. In and out of it all rowed the bumboatmen, local traders approaching moored ships to offer their motley collection of wares, which included everything from provisions, tackle and clothes to 'the services of ladies'. There was also the purl-man, ringing his bell to sell a mulled ale – made, like absinthe, from wormwood – that was popular with sailors and labourers for centuries.

Increasingly, the city's wharves were unable to keep pace with the rapid growth in overseas trade, and ships were left with no option but to moor midstream. So 'lighters' – the smaller barges that lightened their loads – ferried goods from ships to the quayside. Steering required oars up to twenty feet long and the lighterman's job was skilled and difficult, particularly on this chaotic stretch of the Thames. The weight of traffic meant frequent delays, jams and collisions, with the river so busy at times that it was said a person could cross from one bank to the other by stepping on decks.

Following the shore west towards the backdrop of Tower Bridge and the City, I passed PRIVATE signs and crumbling, disused stairs leading through to bricked-up alleyways. There were occasional traces of old docks and wharves on the foreshore: a few blackened timbers from jetties that once served riverside warehouses, and the odd strikingly white pebble eroded from the packed chalk of old barge beds or 'hards', which at low tide prevented the beached ships from sinking in the mud.

Not long after coming down onto the shore, I'd picked up a small piece of coral, something that's relatively common at Wapping. Pale and intricately patterned – and impossibly exotic on the muddy foreshore – this was a reef-building coral native to the warm, clear waters of the Caribbean. Like much of the coral that washes up along the Thames, it was likely to have been dumped as part of the ballast from merchant sailing ships. As their tall masts and great sails made the ships top-heavy, large quantities of ballast were needed to prevent capsize in heavy seas. In the absence of a sufficiently weighty cargo, sand and stones would be collected at the port of origin – men shovelling gravel from the Thames were known as 'ballast-getters' and those filling holds as 'ballast-heavers'.

By the second half of the eighteenth century, the increase in London's seaborne trade was phenomenal. As a result, its wharves became so overstretched that ships were kept waiting for weeks with their goods on board, leaving them vulnerable to thieves. London Bridge was as far as tall-masted ships could go and this stretch of river below it – known as the Pool of London – became notorious. Inadequate warehousing resulted in goods being left piled on quaysides and as lightermen were responsible for their cargo, they frequently slept on board to protect it.

Crime on the Thames soared, both highly organized and opportunistic, and some of the many 'classes of thieves' are described in Peter Ackroyd's *Thames: Sacred River*.

> There were 'river pirates', armed thieves who at night cut the mooring ropes of lighters and waited for them to drift upon the banks or foreshore. There were 'night plunderers', watermen who worked under the cover of darkness, and 'scuffle hunters' or 'long apron men' who specialised in stealing the goods left on the quaysides. There were 'light horsemen' who were the renegade mates of ships and revenue officers, and 'heavy horsemen', the porters and labourers earning a second living.

As London's reputation worsened, approaching ships began to tie or nail down their hatches from Gravesend, twenty miles downriver. By then, Wapping already had a long association with crimes committed both on the river and at sea, and in John Stow's 1598 *Survey of London* it is described as 'the usuall place of execution for hanging of Pirats & sea Rovers'. Although the exact location of Execution Dock is no longer known, the hangings took place at low tide from a gallows on Wapping's foreshore, as in Britain the strip of land between the high and low watermark remained under the jurisdiction of the Admiralty rather than the Crown. Thousands of Londoners would turn out to watch, with men, women and children lining the river or hiring boats for a better view, as pirates were hanged from a shorter rope than usual so that, rather than breaking their neck in the fall, they died more painfully from asphyxiation. According to Stow, after death the bodies would then be chained to a stake, 'at the low water marke, there to remaine, till three tides had overflowed them'. Later, they were smeared with pitch and hung from gibbets at visible points along the river, to serve as a warning to the crews of passing ships.

Dire crime rates made the need for more secure commercial docks urgent, and as work began, their unprecedented scale transformed the landscape of the river. As well as the new East and West India Docks downstream, by 1805 inland Wapping had been hollowed out to provide anchorage for up to 300 sailing ships. Surrounded by fifty acres of warehousing, the docks boasted twenty acres of wine cellars, a 'great wool floor' and a five-acre tobacco warehouse. Two decades on, Wapping Docks was joined by the neighbouring St Katharine Docks, the only one of London's docks to have survived. Reached through a gap in the river wall ahead of me, it is now a luxury marina, recently redeveloped to attract more superyachts. To make way for it in 1825, the ancient district of 'St Katharine's by the Tower' was pulled down, taking with it a maze of narrow lanes and alleyways in the shadow of the Tower of London – amongst them Dark Entry, Cat's Hole and Shovel Alley. At the time this was deeply controversial, as it involved the eviction of a community of more than 10,000 people, the majority of them poor and given no compensation or alternative accommodation.

Three years after the evictions, the new St Katharine Docks opened, specializing in wool and tea as well as luxury goods such as silk and porcelain. With growing demand for exotic imports, the docks were also at the centre of the trade in ivory, ostrich feathers and live turtles. At the time, turtle shells were not only used as 'tortoiseshell' to make ornamental items such as combs and tea caddies, but amongst the wealthy the 'turtle feast' had also acquired a mythical status. With a shell reaching up to eight feet in length, the turtle's 'salubrious' and 'exceedingly sweet' flesh – served mainly at private dinners in gentleman's clubs – embodied prestige and exotic luxury. Eaten initially by seamen on merchant-sailing voyages, it was also a symbol of maritime power and the limitless possibility of empire. At the peak of the trade, 15,000 green sea turtles a year were being shipped live from the West Indies to London, with the price rising steadily as these magnificent creatures were hunted to near extinction.

By the time my ancestors lived at Bluegate Fields, the neighbouring docks were heaving. Nineteenth-century engravings show crowds of workers loading and unloading beneath dense forests of masts and rigging. Wharves were crowded with sailors and dockworkers: riggers and shipwrights, timber-lumpers, corn-porters and coal-whippers. Visitors described quaysides piled with tanned hides and tea chests, bales of cloth and rubber, 'hogsheads' of tobacco and casks of brandy and wine, and everything from elephant tusks and whalebone to ambergris. Warehouse floors were sticky with leaked sugar, the dockside air thick with the scent of cut timber, coffee, spices and rum – and the stench of skins (it was said that in thick fog the older lightermen could navigate the docks by smell alone). In Blanchard Jerrold's 1872 book *London: A Pilgrimage*, descriptions of the docks accompany Gustave Doré's shadowy engravings.

> There is no end to it! London Docks, St Katharine's Docks, Commercial Docks on the other side – India Docks, Victoria Docks; black with coal, blue with indigo, brown with hides, white with flour; stained with purple wine – or brown with tobacco! The perspective of the great entrepôt or warehouse before us is broken and lost in the whirl and movement. Bales, baskets, sacks, hogsheads, and waggons stretch as far as the eye can reach . . . We thread our way round the busy basins, through bales and bundles and grass-bags, over skins and rags, and antlers, ores and dye-woods.

By then, London was the largest and wealthiest city in the world.

An hour or two later, I was absorbed in my search at the far end of the shore when there was a splashing and commotion from the river wall. I looked up to see a man scramble through, wet to the knees and carrying a dog.

'Jesus.' He looked at me with relief. 'I mistimed that a bit. Came down at the Prospect of Whitby . . . thought there'd be more ways up.' He put the dog down and rubbed its wet head, before heading off to the stairs.

The tide had reached the stones now and was coming in fast. As the strip of shore narrowed, the river walls seemed to grow taller. Reflecting the tidal range of the Thames, these were green with weed to the height of a two-storey building. Although the stairs were an easy way out, when you stood near the walls there was something unsettling in knowing that in an hour the water would be above head height. It was also a reminder of just how much the city has constrained the Thames. Already – and it wasn't even half tide – this was a different river. No longer placid and withdrawn, it was on the make. Where the walls were built further out into the river, the strengthening currents were already pushing past their constraints, shouldering up against concrete and stone.

I watched the shore slip slowly underwater, returning to riverbed as the opaque Thames closed over relics it had so briefly revealed. A river bus passed then, with a surge of wake, and I lurched backwards as cold water seeped into a sock. It was time to go. With a series of waves washing up the causeway and breaking over the lower steps, I retreated to the top.

As I hadn't wanted to rush at Wapping, I'd planned the walk to span two low tides – although with twelve hours between them I'd had to wait until May for enough daylight. So, much later that afternoon, I sat drinking coffee at the top of Bankside Stairs, impatient for the tide to fall as I didn't want to lose the light before reaching Water Street. I'd first rooted about on the foreshore here twenty-five years ago, missing the sea once I lived in London, yet it was only a few months earlier that I'd found my first lead token. It wasn't far from the bottom of these steps, the grey rim wedged side-on between stones. On easing it free I found the soft metal was worn and crudely made, with just a trace of what I hoped was the outline of an anchor. On a later visit to the Finds Liaison Officer at the Museum of London, it was confirmed as a late-eighteenth-century trade token, dateable to 1787 or later from the style of the 'fouled' anchor (its added curve of rope becoming common once it was used as the symbol of the Navy). Trade tokens are often found in the Thames, and were used periodically in Britain whenever there was a shortage of small-denomination coins. A lack of change made everyday transactions difficult, so a common solution was for merchants and shopkeepers to provide their own.

As the tokens could only be exchanged for local goods or services, they are commonly found close to the site of the business that issued them. Their designs were also often relevant to the particular trader – at the museum I was told mine was likely to have been issued by someone trading in nautical goods 'or by a tavern called the Anchor'. Only a few hundred yards from where I found the token stands the Anchor pub. So although I'd passed this many times without a thought, it was only then that I began to wonder about its history.

Like low-lying Wapping, the eyots and rural marshland south of the Thames were much slower to develop than the city and retained a very different character. From medieval times Southwark had remained outside the jurisdiction of the City, acquiring a reputation as a lawless sanctuary for criminals. Bankside in particular was well known for its brothels, or 'stews', and in 1598 John Stow recorded some of their names: Beares Heade, the Crosse Keyes, the Gunne, the Cardinals Hatte, the Swanne and the Castle. And one of the first things I learned about the Anchor pub was that it stands on the site of the old Castle – or, to give it its full name, the Castle Upon the Hope Inn. One of Bankside's more notorious brothels, the inn had its own wharf so watermen could land customers ferried over from the City.

Through those centuries, as London spread to poorer ground south of the river, the surrounding marshes were steadily being drained and reclaimed. I was born in Lambeth, a mile or so west around the bend in the river, and there is a sense of that lost landscape in the names of its medieval villages, Waterlambyth and Lambythmarshe. As a child growing up on the Isle of Sheppey in the Thames Estuary, I was told that I'd been born at the General Lion Inn. I asked no more about this and always presumed it was a Lambeth pub. Years later, though, I discovered my mum had actually said General Lying-In – 'lying-in' being an archaic term for bed-rest after childbirth – which turned out to be the maternity annex of St Thomas's Hospital. Like so much else in the area, the hospital stands on land reclaimed from the river, so I was quite pleased to realize that I'd come into the world on what was once the muddy foreshore of that wider, shallower Thames.

At last, the tide was low enough to make it worth heading down onto the shore. As the chatter and noise of passers-by drifted away above me, it was a relief to slip so easily out of the city. With the tide still relatively high, I headed first for the strandline, where the Thames had left its usual chance array of the modern, the ancient and the mysterious. Today, amongst the centuries-old leather and bones was a plastic coffee stirrer, a gritty circuit board and a small silver gas canister. (For some time I'd been finding these canisters regularly and learned recently that while officially used to whip cream, the 'laughing gas' they contain is now Britain's fourth most widely-used recreational drug.)

After making my way slowly along the line of damp flotsam, just before the end I caught sight of something I'd found once before. It was a fragment of bone with a deeply scalloped edge: the distinctive waste material from making bone buttons or beads by hand. I fished around in my finds bag for a fairly nondescript button I'd picked up earlier. When I'd dropped it in the bag wet I wasn't sure if it was bone or plastic, but now could see it was bone. The surface was smooth and worn, and I imagined a heavy coat repeatedly buttoned and unbuttoned. For me there is something evocative in these old, finger-worn buttons. In the past – particularly amongst the poor with their careful conservation of materials – it was common for people to cut the buttons from worn-out clothes and reuse them many times. So it was quite possible that this plain bone button had fastened the clothes of successive generations.

I held it against the bone offcut, where each half-circle was the space where a disc had been removed. Button-making techniques changed little from late medieval times until the nineteenth century's shift to machines, so these offcuts are practically impossible to date. The inner curves were beautifully smooth and, as with the nails at Wapping, I was struck by the deft idiosyncrasies of the manual craftsmanship.

Bone artefacts are common finds on the foreshore. As well as being versatile and readily available, bone could also be polished to resemble more expensive materials like ivory. Over the years, Thames mudlarks have turned up everything from Neolithic fishhooks and Roman hairpins to Victorian tooth-brushes and a wonderful set of 'loaded' medieval bone dice. One of my own favourites is the bone comb in the kitchen cupboard. And on a recent visit to the Finds Liaison Officer, I'd taken along a piece of flat but unremarkable bone on the off-chance it might be something of interest. Pointing out fine marks I could barely see, he said it was similar to the waste he'd seen from the production of bone corset-stays.

'Bone,' he'd said then. 'The plastic of its day.'

For as well as being a cheap by-product of butchery, bone was light, strong and easy to work, so was used for all kinds of objects that today are made from plastic.

I headed further down the shore, setting off along the strip of wet stones at the water's edge. In the late sunlight, their colours were rich. I wandered, trying not to look for anything specific, instead waiting for something to catch my eye. In its constant rearrangement, this glistening strip of shore can be both magical and frustrating. At times in the past, with pleasure boats out on the river, just as I've reached for something their wake has rushed up the shore and swept it away. Sometimes it was just beyond the tips of my fingers, other times I had no more than a fleeting glimpse – or perhaps just a hopeful imagining. When the wave retreated it was gone, conjured away or turned over and nowhere to be seen.

This time I swore I saw a wig curler. I snatched for it, but too late, and the brown Thames rushed up my arm and soaked my sleeve. The crowded boat slipped away downriver, as cold water again seeped in through a sock. There was no sign at all of a wig curler, or of anything even remotely similar: a flint nodule, perhaps, or the pale, worn bowl of a pipe. This last was a mistake I'd made before, as the curlers were made from the same fine clay as the pipes, although it's far more unusual to find one. They were used to curl the notoriously elaborate powdered wigs that so often characterize – and satirize – the Georgian era.

I've found buttons from that time on the foreshore, although they've all been plain: the kind that decorated frock coats. But far more ornate Georgian accessories do emerge from the Thames mud. Very occasionally these cufflinks, buttons or shoe buckles are silver or set with precious stones, worn by London's aristocracy in a display of wealth. More often, though, they are cheaper imitations; equally flamboyant, but pewter or brass set with coloured-glass 'paste stones'. As the middle classes expanded through the eighteenth century, London society was becoming more stratified, allowing wider social mobility with all its unsettling of traditional hierarchies. As an obvious indicator of status, perhaps newfound, owning and wearing the right things was becoming increasingly important.

With more time and money for leisure, the same was true of fashionable habits, which brought with them a range of new forms of consumption. Along with the 'dry drunkenness' of smoking, trade with the New World had introduced Londoners to the caffeinated pleasures of coffee ('their soot-coloured ninny-broth'), hot chocolate and tea. By the Georgian era, coffee houses had been around for a while, but drinking tea was becoming increasingly popular and would go on to take the country by storm. To begin with, many feared addiction to these new, exotic hot drinks. One pamphlet described tea drinking as 'one of the worst of habits, rendering you lost to yourself', and claimed tea houses were frequented by 'loose women' and 'boys whose morals are depraved, and their constitutions ruined'. Yet tea drinking was on the rise in wealthy homes, particularly among groups of women. And all sorts of paraphernalia accompanied the ritual of taking tea. Dainty cups (without handles until the mid eighteenth century) were laid out on silver tea trays, beside ornate teapots and elegant silverware, with the expensive sugar shown off as a luxury by the host. The tea itself was so valuable that at first it was locked away in tea chests, and fashionable ivory or turtle-shell tea caddies.

Some of the most desirable tea sets were made from Chinese porcelain. When compared to Europe's rougher earthenware pottery, the porcelain was impossibly fine. It was delicate, translucent when held up to the light and 'resonant when struck'. Imported from China along with tea and silk, its recipe and manufacturing process remained a closely guarded state secret, with foreign traders kept far from areas where the craftsmen worked. As Londoners grew wealthier, demand for these oriental luxuries continued to rise, yet the Chinese had no interest in buying British goods in return. Instead they wanted payment in silver, which for Britain meant a trade imbalance. The solution, pioneered by the East India Company, was to get farmers in India to grow opium, often against their will. The opium was then smuggled into China on a lucrative 'middle leg' in exchange for Chinese silver – despite the horrors of opium addiction being well understood in Europe at the time.

The East India Company's monopoly on imports helped keep tea so expensive that at first only the wealthy could afford to drink it. From the 1720s, though, the price began to fall and its popularity broadened. In bringing profit to the Empire, tea drinking was heavily promoted by both government and industry, as a civilizing and patriotic habit. Yet in efforts to gain from its rising popularity, the government also began hiking the tax on tea – until by 1750 this had reached an intolerable 119 per cent. In response, a huge tea-smuggling industry grew up, which at its height was using well-armed gangs to run tea from Europe to England's south and east coasts. As with today's illicit drugs, by the time the smuggled tea reached the public it was often adulterated – with dried willow, blackthorn and ash leaves, or used tea leaves that had been re-dried. This did, though, keep the price of the smuggled tea down, which along with later tax reductions on the legal tea brought it within reach of the working classes (taken with bread and drunk with plenty of sugar, it made a cheap substitute for a hot meal).

By the 1840s, when the Tolladays lived at Water Street, tea was drunk across the English social spectrum. In the new indus-trial age it was seen as a respectable and wholesome habit, with factory owners in particular keen to have a sober workforce. Brewed in everything from silver teapots to cans on stoves outside the workplace, this exotic leaf – and bittersweet drink – had become part of British national identity. Perhaps unsurprisingly, then, my collection of shore finds reflects a century or two of English tea drinking: elegant china teacup handles, the lid from a silver sugar bowl – with a slot for the silver spoon – a rusted enamel teapot and a fair collection of tarnished teaspoons (in the 1700s, as the price of tea and sugar came down, these grew in size from a quarter to a third of a tablespoon).

As it was Friday evening the party boats were out in force now, their wake regularly surging up the shore towards me. While frustrating at times, there is also something I love in this. Within its rush of sound – the watery slap against posts, the drag of stones in the backwash – there is a scattering of glassy high notes. I remember when I noticed this for the first time, as it was something I never heard on sea beaches. Listening to the sound retreat along the foreshore with a wave, I'd imagined bone china clinking against flint and broken glass. Back home, while swirling a tub of soaking finds with my hand, I'd realized it was the clay pipes that made the musical high notes.

In the bag now were a few lengths of their river-worn stems, stained a soft grey by the mud, and several bowls with quite different shapes. Because their design evolved steadily over the 300 years they were popular, clay pipes are closely dateable. Which means that in the curves of their china-clay bowls – so beautifully preserved by the mud – lie traces of the cultural and economic changes that swept Britain through those centuries of merchant capitalism and then industrialization.

When first introduced to Tudor England, tobacco was rare and expensive. So the very first pipes – dating from around 1580 – are so tiny they are known as fairy pipes. Like a seventeenth-century pipe I'd found earlier, those that followed had small, hand-shaped bulbous bowls, and were passed around by wealthy men said to be 'drinking smoke'. Through the following century, as trade increased and the price of tobacco fell, this was reflected in the increasing size of the bowls. They lengthened and became more elegant; some rested on a narrow spur. From 1680 to 1700, millions were produced, often by small family businesses (once the poor could afford to smoke, too, the wealthy moved on to French snuff). With the invention of the vicelike 'gin' (short for engine) press, production rates rose significantly; the bowl walls became thinner and designs more elaborate. My own pipes that day were all plain, but others came out of the moulds shaped as everything from human skulls and reclining women to African faces and turbaned Turks' heads.

By the time my male ancestors were pipemakers in the 1800s

– and their wives 'pipe-trimmers' – industrialization was changing the job, as smaller home workshops closed down and production became more centralized in larger factories. By then, as the vast number of clay pipes in the Thames suggests, for generations they'd been considered more or less disposable. Often used to promote businesses, they were given away free by taverns with pouches of tobacco – to be smoked a handful of times, or perhaps only once, before being thrown away. In this, they remain a rather beautiful precursor of the plastic bottles and single-use forks I find on the foreshore with them.

Like the growth in the size of the bowls, the vast number of discarded clay pipes also reflected the falling price of tobacco – which was the result of slavery reaching American plantations. Something else I'd picked up on the Wapping foreshore was the shell of a money cowrie. They are so-called as this species was once a form of currency used across the world (another, from the scientific genus *Spondylus*, is said to be the origin of the eighteenth-century slang term for money, 'spondoolicks'). Money cowries are not native to Britain and the reason they turn up in the Thames is their use as 'hard cash' in West Africa. In the eighteenth century, cowrie shells were a major commodity imported by the British, collected in vast quantities from islands and atolls in the Indian Ocean. On the journey to England they would be used as ballast and also – rather like today's polystyrene 'packing peanuts' – to fill space around fragile goods such as Chinese porcelain.

From England, most of the cowries were then shipped to Africa, on a first leg of the triangular routes of the slave trade. These ships also carried cloth, iron bars, brandy, tobacco, guns and ammunition – anything that could be bartered with local traders and brokers. On reaching West Africa, the imported goods would be exchanged for gold, ivory and slaves – in the mid 1700s, one enslaved African could be bought for 25,000 cowrie shells. The slaves, many captured by middlemen in armed raids on inland settlements, were then shackled and crammed into holds for the notoriously cruel 'middle passage'. Lasting months, sometimes four or more in bad weather, conditions below deck on these journeys were so appalling that up to one in five died at sea. On reaching the Caribbean – the New World – those slaves who did survive were then sold on to plantation owners in exchange for cargoes of rum, sugar and tobacco.

By the eighteenth century, slaves were increasingly being sold to work on sugar plantations, as this 'white gold' had become Britain's most valuable commodity. In *The Sugar Barons*, Matthew Parker describes the colonists living on Caribbean islands far from their native England, making fortunes beyond their wildest dreams. Visitors described being struck by the decadence of their parties, by their extravagant clothes, drunkenness and debauchery – and by the sadistic cruelty shown to slaves.

In the cane-fields and boiling houses, the Africans' work was both backbreaking and dangerous; already weakened by the journey, another third died within three years of arrival. Punishments were brutal and often degrading, and included severe floggings, mutilation and execution. Visitors arriving on the islands 'fresh from England' would be shocked to find slaves starving in gibbets with a loaf of bread hung just out of reach, or their decapitated heads displayed on stakes as a warning to others. But if these newcomers stayed, it was said they generally acclimatized, coming to accept the usual justifications of slavery: that it was essential for the economy of certain industries, that a race could be 'naturally inferior' and 'not fully human'.

Through another find I learned that back in London – before being shown off at tea in wealthy homes – the hot, raw sugar would be drained in moulds at one of the city's many refineries. The Museum of London's Finds Liaison Officer took one look at the fairly nondescript terracotta ring I showed him and said it was the drain-hole from a seventeenth-century sugar mould. He described their tall, conical shape in the air and said the refined white sugar was then sold in the shops as 'sugarloaves'.

By the eighteenth century, the sugar and tobacco industries were so vast that most English investors and merchants had some involvement with slavery. As a result the sugar and tobacco lobbies were powerful within government, so despite a growing anti-slavery movement amongst the British population from the 1780s, lobbyists helped delay its abolition for decades. By the time the Slavery Abolition Act was passed in 1833, the trade had enslaved more than 11 million Africans and led to the deaths of an estimated 4 million. On the African continent, it left a legacy of devastated communities, destabilized kingdoms and wars.

It was just beginning to get dark. Concerned about losing the light before reaching Water Street, I headed for the nearest steps. Halfway up I paused to rummage amongst the day's finds for the coral and the cowrie, just to be sure they were there. They were, and as I stood looking out at the retreating tide, their journey from clear, tropical waters to the mud of the Thames seemed as telling as any of my man-made finds. During those centuries of expanding empire and seaborne trade, so much in Britain had changed, especially for the new middle classes: in the ways they lived and the things they could buy. Many more could now aspire to the latest fashions – to porcelain teapots, ivory-handled cutlery and turtle-shell tea caddies. This was particularly true in London since – as can be glimpsed amongst the foreshore rubble – through a combination of geographical luck, empire, slavery and coal reserves, Britain had found itself at the forefront of an unprecedented rise in consumption. And with reputations and so much money to be made, it was easy to overlook the human and environmental costs of large-scale production and those distant trades, from the brutal cruelty of slavery to colonial plunder and the hunting of species to near extinction. I wiped the cowrie clean and sat it in the palm of my hand. Cold, shiny and hard, it was heavy with association.

2

South Bank to Water Street

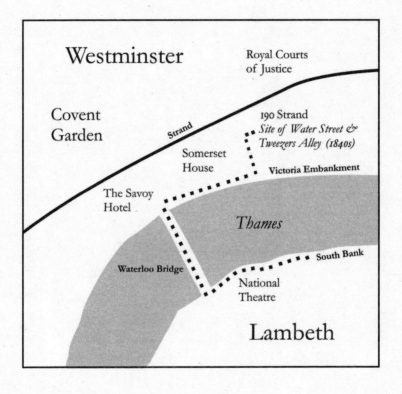

Westminster

Royal Courts
of Justice

Covent
Garden

Strand

190 Strand
Site of Water Street &
Tweezers Alley (1840s)

Somerset
House

Victoria Embankment

The Savoy
Hotel

Thames

South Bank

Waterloo Bridge

National
Theatre

Lambeth

As I approached the South Bank's concrete National Theatre, I was opposite Water Street, separated by little more than a brassy expanse of river. Although another nearby street has the name today, I'd learned from earlier maps that when the Tolladays lived there in 1841 it ran from the Thames waterfront up to the Strand. Looking out to it now across the water, much of the area was unfinished blocks. With the working week over, the raising of the city was on hold: huge cranes crouched on their rooftops, delicate at a distance, not moving their crane-fly limbs.

This would be the first time I'd tried to find Water Street, but back in Cornwall, as I waited for the days to lengthen, I'd begun to research the area. In the 1840s it was in the ancient parish of St Clement Danes, which no longer exists but took its name from both the patron saint of sailors and the Vikings who settled there after the Saxon retreat. From medieval times, the Strand had been the main thoroughfare, the name derived from the Old Norse *strond*, meaning shore, as originally it was a track along the banks of a wider Thames. Back in the twelfth century, the street was lined with riverside mansions: the townhouses of dukes, bishops and earls. By the 1840s, though, the aristocracy had moved on to the West End, and the street was one of Georgian townhouses, taverns and shop fronts, crowded with hackney carriages, carts and horse-drawn buses.

Ten minutes later I was up on Waterloo Bridge, suspended

between the two halves of the modern city, making it easier to picture St Clement Danes as it was. Then, as in other parts of the city, the wealthy, impressive facades of main streets hid dense pockets of cramped and dilapidated housing: mazes of courts and alleyways grown up over centuries. With the gathering pace of industrialization, London's population was soaring. At just over half a million in 1700, by 1800 it had doubled to a million; by 1841 it had already doubled again. This was now the most populous city in the world, and until then no one had tried packing more than 2 million people inside a thirty-mile circumference.

Most of the growth was the result of migration from elsewhere in Britain, generally from the countryside. As well as the draw of better-paid work, the 'enclosure movement' had gathered pace, ending ancient open-farming systems where tenant farmers lived off common land. Young people in particular were arriving in London in their thousands every year, seeking opportunity and 'betterment' in the city. In 1707 it was said that for any son or daughter of an English family 'that exceeds the rest in beauty, or wit, or perhaps courage, or industry, or any other rare quality, London is their North star'.

Yet while industrialization brought rising wealth and vast fortunes for some, for many more, things didn't work out as they'd hoped. The work available was often casual and insecure – every morning at the docks, hundreds or thousands of men queued for a day or a half-day's work, with the majority turned away. In leaving their homes in the countryside, people were also leaving behind any safety net of family or parish support, making it easier to spiral into poverty. In the slums of St Clement Danes, out of sight of the bustling commerce of the Strand, the poorest lived in desperately overcrowded squalor.

As centuries of mercantilism gave way to industrialization, the human and environmental costs had moved closer to home. The Industrial Revolution, with its new forms of energy and capital, had triggered rapid population growth, and yet early Victorian London was still functioning with no more than Elizabethan public infrastructure. This was particularly true of how the city dealt with the vast amount of waste its population now produced, which was having a devastating impact on society – both in the ways people lived and how they died. It was something that became grimly clear as I learned more about the places where my own family had lived.

Walking past stationary Friday night traffic, I had a clear view of the Victoria Embankment below, of the modern pier with its cruisers and party boats. It had taken me a while to work out the line of the waterfront when the Tolladays lived there. From the very beginning, as London's population grew and its land increased in value, the river walls had been extended ever further out into the Thames, and with each encroachment the river narrowed and ran deeper and faster. As the Victorian era brought so much change to the waterfront with the new embankments, I'd had to go back through several wonderfully detailed maps engraved in the eighteenth and nineteenth centuries. A favourite resource was the British Library website, where the old maps can be overlaid with their modern equivalents. An onscreen slider fades seamlessly between these snapshots of the past and present, which is both fascinating and oddly compelling. I found myself doing this over and over again – sometimes fast, sometimes slow – watching as the clean lines of the modern city slipped away and the ghosts of old streets emerged.

I found the shifting banks of the Thames particularly addictive. Sliding back through two centuries, the widening river erases the hard edges of modern office blocks, roads and embankments. In places, the old waterfront was 150 metres inland of where it is today, and early Victorian paintings show the river shelving gently to a muddy foreshore. It was also lined with watermen's stairs, and on the 1799 map their names fan out across the water in elegant lettering: Pickleherring Stairs, Horse Shoe Alley Stairs, Dog & Duck Stairs, Goat Stairs. At the bottom of Water Street were Arundel Stairs, which in medieval times served the riverside palace of Arundel House, townhouse of the Bishops of Bath and Wells. By the 1840s, though, the stairs were surrounded by coal wharves.

Having followed the family back through generations of dustmen and coalmen, I'd been surprised to find that in 1841 my third great-grandfather, William Tolladay, was a bookbinder living off the Strand. On learning this, I'd pored over the mottled pages of that year's census, tracing the route of the 'census enumerator' through neighbouring streets leading up to the Strand. In a confident, sloping hand he had recorded the street's shopkeepers – confectioner, hatter, tobacconist, tailor – before returning to the riverside streets and alleyways hidden behind, where the Tolladays lived. At the time, people usually lived close to their place of work, and their Water Street neighbours included watermen, lightermen, a milliner, a coal merchant and coal porters.

Of Water Street itself I could find no images, but Milford Lane, running parallel, seems to have attracted more attention. A nineteenth-century drawing and engraving show a shadowy cobbled street, the backs of houses and smoking chimneys, and a narrow entrance onto the Strand. I'd read that by the seventeenth century the area had a reputation as a hiding place for debtors, and found several references to Milford Lane brothels (the most bizarre a poem by the sixth Earl of Dorset, recounting a battle fought between armies of lice in the pubic hair of a Milford Lane prostitute). Around the same time, John Strype, in his update of *Stow's Survey of London*, described the street as 'a Place much pestered with Carts and Carrs, for the bringing of Coals and other Goods from the Wharfs by the Water side . . . and therefore ill-inhabited, with old Buildings'.

By the time the Tolladays lived there, similar coal wharves were found throughout the city, and the blackened brigs and barges bringing coal from the north of England were a common sight on the Thames. The previous century's invention of the coal-fired steam engine had been a turning point. For tens of thousands of years our power had come mainly from muscles, both human and animal, but as those with the muscles needed feeding, power was limited by the land available to grow food and fodder, and the annual cycle of photosynthesis. Now, in going below ground, at first for coal and later for oil and gas, we were able to release the energy trapped in fossil fuels. This was energy from the sun, captured through photosynthesis millions of years earlier – the coal from decaying plant material, and oil and gas from plankton and other marine organisms that drifted to the floor of ancient seas. With the invention of the steam engine, harnessing that captured sunlight to do the work of dozens of horses, we broke free of those constraints. It was this radical shift in energy sources that unleashed the Industrial Revolution, driving technological, economic and social change.

By the 1840s, with the rapid expansion in the use of steam engines, coal was needed in ever greater quantities. Increasingly powerful engines and the new machine tools had brought unprecedented growth in industrial output, a major draw for the large numbers of agricultural workers flocking to London to work in the factories. Other coal-fired modernizations included the new 'coal-gas' street lighting and household cooking stoves. Coal would also go on to power the new steamships: freed from their reliance on energy from wind and currents, merchant ships could then travel wherever and whenever they wanted.

Coal had also entered ordinary homes and, by the end of the decade, the average London household was burning an estimated eleven tonnes of it every year. With the rise of fossil fuels, the city's air might be thick with its infamous – and deadly – pea-souper smogs, but the potential for growth seemed limitless. As merchants, shipowners and industrialists amassed fortunes to rival those of the aristocracy, the Victorian middle classes continued to expand, inspired by popular narratives of hard work, self-reliance and personal success. Yet such new aspirations also had a darker side, allowing the successful to see poverty as the fault of the poor themselves: a result of their lack of effort.

To many, the lowest of the low were the city's scavengers. (A century later, my nan considered my grandad's job as a dustman a big step up from his dad's scavenging – although when my mum married, she still told her not to write 'dustman' as her dad's occupation, but instead to put 'refuse collector'. Unused to the phrase, my mum wrote 'refuge collector', causing the vicar to ask '*refugee* collector?') In 1840s London, with so many living in poverty, the city's burgeoning waste presented an opportunity, and it is thought that more than 100,000 scavenged a living from its streets, sewers and riverbanks. For outside the city's more official system of the 'dustyard', an unplanned system of recycling had grown up, supplying complex underground markets. This meant that most of London's scavengers specialized. As Stephen Johnson wrote in *The Ghost Map*, a history of the city's 1854 cholera epidemic, 'Just the names alone read now like some kind of exotic zoological catalogue: bone-pickers, rag-gatherers, pure-finders, dredgermen, mud-larks, sewer-hunters, dustmen, night-soil men, bunters, toshers and shoremen.'

With no state pension and a widespread fear of the new workhouses, scavenging was often a last resort for those who would otherwise be destitute. Mudlarks in particular could be desperately poor and were often children, the widowed or the elderly. Looking down now at the Thames pressing up against sheer embankment walls, I felt in my pocket for the small, tide-worn piece of coal I'd picked up earlier on the shore. In the nineteenth century, the foreshore around coal wharves – as at the bottom of Water Street – was particularly popular with mudlarks. In 1851 Henry Mayhew, journalist and author of *London Labour and the London Poor*, described a group he met:

> Their bodies are grimed with the foul soil of the river, and their torn garments stiffened up like boards . . . It is indeed pitiable to behold them, especially during the winter . . . paddling and groping among the wet mud for small pieces of coal, chips of wood, or any sort of refuse washed up by the tide.

They searched the shore for anything that could be sold to street dealers, known as 'dollies' after the black wooden dolls that hung over the doors of shops they supplied. Along with the coals and wood – which were bought by the poor as fuel – mudlarks also collected rope, metal and glass, sometimes bones, and occasionally something as valuable as a coin. Some street dealers had a barrow or donkey and cart, and, like the scavengers, most of them specialized: in crockery and glass, scrap metal, or rags and old clothes. Other options were to sell to the rag-and-bone men, to rag-and-bottle shops or the more general 'marine stores'. These were the 'dolly shops', part junk shop and part pawnshop, offering what Charles Dickens described as 'the most extraordinary and confused jumble of old, worn-out, wretched articles'.

Amongst the city's scavengers, it was the toshers – known also as shore-men or sewer-hunters – who considered themselves scavenger aristocracy. They would sometimes search the shore or visit rubbish dumps, but mostly they entered the sewers at night. Henry Mayhew met a number known only by nickname – Long Tom, Short-armed Jack, One-eyed George – and estimated that at the time more than 200 made a living in London's sewers.

> Habited in long greasy velveteen coats, furnished with pockets
> of vast capacity . . . they provide themselves, in addition, with
> a canvas apron, which they tie round them, and a dark lantern
> similar to a policeman's . . . They carry a bag on their back,
> and in their left hand a pole.

Dropping the coal back in my own capacious pocket, I was
sharply aware of the difference between mudlarking today and
scraping together enough money from finds to eat or feed a
family.

The toshers' work in particular was both grim and dangerous.
Along with myths of mutant rats and sewer-pigs, there were
also the very real risks of being trapped by rising tides or of
causing an explosion – which happened when their lamps'
naked flames ignited methane produced by the sewage. Primarily,
the toshers were after scrap metal, or lost valuables such as
jewellery or coins that might have washed down drains. Copper
was particularly valuable, and 'tosh' – before its more recent
meaning of rubbish – was originally anything made of copper.
To the dustmen of my grandad's generation, half a crown was
still known as a 'tosheroon'.

Bone-grubbers worked the streets collecting animal bones,
which were sold on to make glue, tallow candles or soap. There
were also the pure-finders: 'pure' was dog faeces used to 'purify'
leather. It was bought by the tanneries for use as an astringent,
and rubbed by hand into specialist leathers such as the calf-skin
used to cover books or make expensive gloves. Collected mainly
from London's streets – some finders Mayhew interviewed wore
a single black-leather glove – the pure would then be carried
in covered baskets to hide the contents.

Rag-gatherers supplied a more complex market, through
the city's vast number of rag merchants and old-clothesmen.
Everything would be carefully picked over. Once any saleable
second-hand clothes had been separated, much of the rest could

be sold on to rugmakers and paper mills, or to upholsterers for use as stuffing. Scraps and seams would be left to rot and then sold as manure, with any leftover wool shredded and sent to the 'shoddy mills'. There it would be re-spun into a coarse cloth known as rag-wool, which was used to make blankets and army uniforms. Any left that was too short to spin would then be baled up and sold to farmers in Kent, where it was dug into hop fields to improve the soil. With so many Londoners living in poverty at the time, nothing was wasted and almost every last scrap had a value.

Although in 1841 this stretch of the Thames was crowded with wharves and watermen's stairs, by the mid 1860s all of that had gone, to be replaced by the vast new embankments.

'Them blessed "bankments",' one elderly mudlark exclaimed to the journalist James Greenwood. In an 1883 *Daily Telegraph* piece, 'Gleaners of Thames Bank', Greenwood described

> a bedraggled, mud-be-spattered creature . . . shoeless and stock-ingless with a coarse sodden sack . . . poking and raking amongst the mud, and between the vessels at the wharves, for bits of coal cast overboard by accident: and there she was ankle-deep in the water and with her skirts dabbling in it, washing the tenacious slime from her gleanings so as to give them a market-able appearance.

She said her elderly husband also worked the shore, 'though not for coals. He takes the shore in general – anything that washes up. Old coins . . . bones and old rope.' Another told the journalist, 'There ain't half the number of larks there used to be, sir, twenty years ago,' and then complained about the 'ferrets' that 'work the shore only for robbery', giving honest mudlarks a bad name.

In the 1840s, there was still enough money in recycling for London's official refuse collectors to be willing to pay for the privilege of collecting it. Local authorities were not yet responsible for rubbish clearance, and amid accusations of monopolies and bribery, 'dust contractors' would bid £1,000 or more to empty a parish's bins and clean its streets. Significant profits could be made because at the time the bulk of household waste was the ash from coal fires, a valuable commodity.

Whereas in the medieval city household waste was often simply thrown out into the street or dumped in the nearest river, there was now so much that it had to be carted out to the newly emerging suburbs – where vast 'dust heaps' had become a striking sight. In E. H. Dixon's 1837 watercolour *The Great Dust Heap*, one looms like a grey mountain over neighbouring houses, with tiny figures at its base and a horse and cart toiling their way to the top. As R. H. Horne wrote in 1850:

> There rose against the muddled-grey sky, a huge Dust-heap of a dirty black colour, being, in fact, one of those immense mounds of cinders, ashes, and other emptyings from dust-holes and bins, which have conferred celebrity on certain suburban neighbourhoods.

A dust contractor or 'master scavenger' owned open carts and a yard, and hired sifters and sorters as well as 'ordinary and pauper scavengers' to work the streets. They also employed dustmen to go house-to-house with a horse and cart. The unofficial uniform included a large fan-tailed hat, with the reverse brim acting as protection against spills from shouldered baskets. Although the dustmen dressed similarly to coalmen, they were easily distinguished: where the coalmen would be black with soot, the dustmen were grey with ash. In Lee Jackson's recent *Dirty Old London*, he describes the city's Victorian dustmen as having a reputation for 'a certain rough-hewn independence and solidarity' and 'a healthy disregard for authority and the general public'. Coupled with the low pay, this led to a system of tipping – some called it blackmail – that was known as a dustman's 'sparrows'. Before the introduction of removable bins, the 'dust-hole' was often only accessible through the house and, if no tip was forthcoming, the dustman was liable to leave 'some trace of his visit on the wall-paper or floor'. (When I mentioned this to my mum she nodded and said it was still common a century later.)

With profits to be made, their rounds also attracted illegal 'running dustmen', who emptied the dust-holes ahead of the regular dustmen. With no connection to a dustyard, after sifting for anything of value, they would then dump the remaining ash on a quiet road or let it spill from the cart.

In the 1840s, while conducting research for *London Labour and the London Poor*, Henry Mayhew spent time at a London dustyard.

> The dustmen are, generally speaking, an hereditary race; when children they are reared in the dust-yard, and are habituated to the work gradually as they grow up . . . In a dust-yard lately visited the sifters formed a curious sight; they were almost up to their middle in dust, ranged in a semi-circle in front of that part of the heap which was being 'worked'; each had before her a small mound of soil which had fallen through her sieve and formed a sort of embankment.

Whereas the dust was 'thrown up' onto the heap by men, the sorters and sifters were often women and children. The women Mayhew met wore leather or sackcloth aprons, fingerless gloves and 'great lace-up boots', while a 'hillwoman' was in charge of their work. As with the unofficial scavenging, any rags, paper, glass and scrap metal would be separated out at the start and sold to dealers who visited the yard. Bricks and broken crockery, along with the city's vast quantity of discarded oyster shells, could be sold on to builders as hardcore to prepare the ground for roads and houses. 'Software' – rotting vegetables and animal matter, along with anything else that would decompose – was either sold as pig food or mixed in with manure. 'Wet bones', those with any fat or marrow, were held back for the soap and tallow boilers or sold to glue factories, with the rest crushed to be used as fertilizer.

Nothing that came into the yard went to waste. Sorters each had their own speciality, and maximizing profit from 'dust' required ingenuity on the part of both buyers and sellers. Old tins and broken kettles could be sold to trunkmakers to make corner clamps, while larger cinders went to braziers and laundresses. Broken glass was bought as 'cullet' for re-melting, or might be crushed and used to make emery paper, and bootmakers took worn-out shoes and leather scraps to use as stuffing between inner and outer soles. There was even a market for dead cats, which were sold to furriers at 'sixpence for a white cat, fourpence for a coloured cat, and for a black one according to her quality'.

Yet it was what remained that made the dustyard viable. The last job was for the sifters to separate the fine ash from the coarser 'breeze' (so-called as it was what remained when the wind blew the dust away). The ash could then be sold as a soil improver for marshy ground or mixed in with road sweepings to sell on as fertilizer. The breeze was bought as fuel by the brick-making industry or, being cheaper than sand, by builders to mix in with mortar.

As a result, almost nothing was left. With so many Londoners desperately poor, resources were valued and there was a market for almost everything. With its great dustyards and armies of unofficial scavengers, the early Victorian city was close to producing zero waste.

Back down at street level, I followed the tree-lined footpath and cut up across riverside gardens. Although this would be my first visit, I already knew that the site of the old Water

Street now lay beneath a new development: a series of eight-storey buildings known collectively as 190 Strand. Yet when I reached them, things were hard to make out; I was too close now to see the rooftop cranes, and scaffolding and hoardings obscured much of the rest. Plastic sheeting flapped above me in the wind and I thought at first that I wouldn't be able to get in – until I saw a sign pointing a way through to parking. It was just beginning to get dark. I felt uneasy entering a building site, but there was no one around so I wandered in. At the end of a short, canyonlike lane the temporary site reception stood empty, lit by glowing computer screens. I passed the open window expecting a head to appear, for someone to call out and ask why I was there, but no one did.

I turned a corner, deep within the site now, and realized I could be on a last fragment of Water Street. It no longer seemed to have a name, yet I knew from modern maps that the new Water Street ran perpendicular to the old. I wasn't sure, though, until I spotted the entrance to Tweezers Alley. This was cordoned off and inaccessible, but its name was still on the wall. I remembered the alley from the 1799 map and all at once could make out the layout of all those lost streets. In 1841, before the Victoria Embankment was built, this was close to the river and the coal wharves. Back in Cornwall, tracing the route taken by the census enumerator, I'd worked out that the Tolladays lived close to Tweezers Alley, which cut through from Water Street to Milford Lane (although at the time of the earl's pubic-lice poem, it seems to have been more commonly known as Pissing Alley).

Here, a stone's throw from the polluted waters of the Thames, my third great-grandmother Ellen would have been almost thirty, caring for two young children and a baby. With William out at work binding books, she would have spent much of her time trying to keep things clean, not least scrubbing the family's clothes and hanging them to dry in smogs that blackened lungs and clung to washing. Coal dust was also inside the home now, from stoves and open fires. Floors needed scrubbing, curtains washing and carpets beating; lacking our own labour-saving machines, the average Victorian worked so hard they needed to eat twice as many calories. Without a fridge, Ellen would also have shopped daily to feed the family, setting off down the street I was standing on to cross the Strand and head for local markets, which at the time sold everything from sheep's heads and eels to second-hand clothes and 'translated' boots (worn-out footwear that was resoled and refronted, with the old leather given a coat of paint: there were often many stages of reuse and renewal before something reached the sorters at the dustyard).

For a while I stood listening to traffic muffled by newly built walls, to people making their way home from work. Later, I looked up 190 Strand to find that Phase One had recently gone on the market as 'a world-class address closely linked to the richest aspects of London living'. In a promotional film the camera sweeps along the Thames to orchestral music, pans down the building's 'laser-cut metal filigree facade' and enters light-filled reception rooms. Elsewhere, an estate agent's brochure described its range of leisure facilities – a luxury pool and spa, private cinema, state-of-the-art fitness suite, virtual golf – and offered three apartments at 5 to 9 million pounds.

I turned to leave, still having seen no one at all on the site. Somehow, now I was there, those vanished Victorian streets felt even further away than before – sealed beneath the great scale of unfinished development. I eased the straps on the rucksack, unsurprised but still faintly disappointed. It was time to get the bus.

I headed upstairs and was pleased to find a window seat, as I hoped to catch a glimpse of where the Tolladays lived after

Water Street. From the 1851 census, I'd learned that they were still in the parish of St Clement Danes, only now at 17 Clements Lane. Here, William was no longer listed as a bookbinder, but a labourer. On Tuesday 8 April there were thirty-nine people living at number 17, with the Tolladays one of seven families. Around that time a journalist visiting the street described 'nearly every room in every house occupied by a different family'. A decade after my first glimpse of them living in Water Street, it seemed William and Ellen now shared a room with six children – the youngest a baby of two weeks.

The street no longer exists and again it took a while to work out where it was. A map from 1868, not two decades later, showed no sign of it. Eventually, from a map published in 1799, I found that Clements Lane ran from Clare Market down to a cluster of courts and alleyways on the north side of the Strand. Originally printed as thirty-two separate engravings, the detail on this map is extraordinary. Not only are individual houses shown, but most are numbered. It also shows that the cramped, labyrinthine passages and alleyways hidden behind main streets stretched for half a mile through central London. From the Strand they ran up past Clements Lane and continued, more or less unbroken, to the notorious slums of St Giles. Just prior to the 1851 census, Thomas Beame had described these in *The Rookeries of London*.

> Turn aside from streets whose shops teem with every luxury and you have scarce gone a hundred yards when you are in *The Rookery*. The change is marvellous: squalid children, haggard men, with long uncombed hair, in rags, most of them smoking, many speaking Irish; women without shoes or stockings – a babe perhaps at the breast, with a single garment, confined to the waist by a bit of string; wolfish-looking dogs . . .

I stared out at the blue dusk, thinking that at this speed at least I'd get a look at what was once Clements Lane. Although the street had initially been hard to locate, unlike Water Street it was easy to find references to it – and I soon learned that by the time it was demolished it was notorious for deeply disturbing reasons.

When the Tolladays lived there, it was at the western edge of the slums. Again I looked for clues in their neighbours' jobs, which now included a costermonger, a chimney sweep, several bricklayers, a 'general agent', a thirteen-year-old servant and a pauper. Several of the other houses on Clements Lane were lodgings or dosshouses, either all male or all female, which was common at the time. Those staying at the neighbouring women's lodgings included needleworkers, charwomen and a straw-bonnetmaker. Along the street, at number 29, amongst the male lodgers were a number of Irish labourers, a 'gentleman' and a tripe dresser. These places often slept several to a room – it was possible to rent just a corner – and they were essential for the city's vast number of casual and itinerant workers, many of them migrants arriving from the countryside.

At its top end, Clements Lane ran into Clare Market. This was the second largest meat market in London, with the area known for its slaughterhouses, tripe factories and offal shops. In his *Dictionary of London*, Charles Dickens described the market's butcher shops as 'filled with strange pieces of coarse, dark-coloured, and unwholesome-looking meat . . . you take it on faith it is the meat of the ox or sheep.' Its narrow, crowded lanes were lined with stalls and barrows, and the din of costermongers haggling with customers: 'Ill-dressed, worn, untidy, and wretched, many of them look, but they joke with their acquaintances.' The market was also known for its many taverns as well as its gin shops, as a century after the devastation of the Gin Craze, 'Mother's Ruin' was again in fashion.

'Don't go alone,' wrote the Victorian journalist George Simms. 'It is a dangerous neighbourhood to strangers.' The mazelike confusion of courts and alleyways around Clements Lane was notorious: 'There is a legend hereabout that years ago a young man from the country, bearing a black bag, started one winter night from Portugal Street to get into the Strand, and that he has been wandering round and about ever since, constantly returning with a disconsolate aspect to his original starting-point. On foggy nights his form may be descried in Clare Market. Anyhow, no one has yet heard that he ever reached the Strand.'

When I first looked up Clements Lane, every reference I found involved the dead. One reason for this was that many of its houses backed onto Green Ground, which had been a burial site since the seventeenth century. Before the Tolladays lived there, the site was described in a letter to *The Times*:

> A notorious ground, and a regular source of corpses for bodysnatchers. In February 1820 three bodies were seen being bundled over the wall. A warrant was issued to search St Thomas's hospital, where the yard and dissecting room 'resembled a slaughter house' with scattered heads, torsos and limbs.

A cause of Green Ground's notoriety was that it featured repeatedly in the campaigning work of the surgeon George Walker. Known as 'Graveyard Walker', he believed an important cause of disease and ill health amongst the poor was graveyard 'miasma' and so spent much of his life campaigning against urban graveyards.

At the time, the miasma theory of disease held sway: a belief that disease was spread by 'bad air' from rotting organic matter, which could be detected by its foul smell. Unsurprisingly, death rates – commonly from fevers, typhus, lung disease, consumption and cholera – were highest in the overcrowded, damp and often filthy conditions of the slums. Toilets were shared by vast numbers of people, and air pollution was appalling as a result of the burning of coal in both homes and factories. Also, as residents couldn't pay the dustmen their 'sparrows', slum neighbourhoods were known by the dustmen as 'dead pieces' and completely ignored. Rubbish and waste were left to accumulate close to where people lived, with makeshift dust-holes overflowing into cellars, cesspits and fetid alleyways.

Of most concern to those living outside the slums were the contagious outbreaks of cholera. Although many felt the poor's susceptibility to cholera was a result of their own moral degeneracy, a major contributor was also thought to be miasma from the cesspits under houses. So by 1847 new laws were brought in, requiring private toilets to be connected to main sewers (although the response of the worst slum landlords was simply to remove the toilets altogether). The result was that the city's sewage now poured straight into the Thames. At the time, much of London's drinking water was piped directly from the river and so, because cholera is waterborne, one tragic result of the new sewers was a *rise* in the number of cholera deaths.

By the middle of the century – with its growing population and soaring death rates – most of London's burial grounds and churchyards were full. There was simply no more room for the dead, and they became another form of refuse with which the city could no longer cope. In the graveyards, coffins were now stacked together in deep shafts, with remains sometimes removed to make room for more. With a good grasp of the power of propaganda, George 'Graveyard' Walker soon realized that the best way to focus public attention would be to publish the grisly details. In *Gatherings from Graveyards* he described the scene from the window of a back attic in Clements Lane.

> . . . two graves open, close to the south-eastern extremity of this burying ground. Several bones were lying on the surface of the grave nearest to us – a large heap of coffin wood was placed in readiness for removal . . . evidently not in a decayed state.

As only the wealthy could afford plots in the new cemeteries on the outskirts of the city, the lack of burial space was yet another problem that was most acute in the poorest neighbourhoods. One distressing result was that after death, many bodies – often still contagious – were kept in the same rooms where families lived, as they tried to raise money for a burial.

The greatest scandal of all was at Enon Chapel (although Enon is a common Baptist name for a spring, this one stood over an open sewer). Midway up Clements Lane, it was primarily a burial speculation, offering an affordable service to the poor. It became George Walker's most notorious example. Opening in 1822, the chapel was built above a burial vault, a common response to the Church's growing fear of body snatchers. For almost two decades, the minister at Enon offered burials at between eight and fifteen shillings – considerably cheaper than his rivals – and business was brisk. Over time, though, locals began to comment on the cellar's surprising capacity. Worshippers also complained about the smell, and what children at the Sunday School called 'body bugs'.

By 1842 thousands of bodies had been 'buried' in Enon's 59-by-12-foot cellar, with some estimates as high as 12,000. Eventually, coffins were found piled to the rafters – inches from the feet of churchgoers above – and later investigations revealed that bodies had also been removed in carts and dumped in the Thames. Others were dissolved in quicklime, with the empty coffins burnt as firewood in the minister's kitchen. Yet when Enon was at last closed down, the dead were left in the vault. Later, the upstairs pews were removed and the hall leased by a temperance society for public lectures and dances, described by Walker as 'quadrilles, waltzes, country-dances, gallopades, reels . . . danced over the masses of mortality in the cellar beneath'. Some advertisements referred to the bodies as promotion: 'Enon Chapel – Dancing on the Dead – Admission Threepence'.

In 1847 Walker took on Enon's lease himself, so as to have the bodies exhumed and reburied. First, though – as part of his campaign against urban burials – the public were invited to view the horrors beneath the dance hall. It seems these events had an element of the fairground sideshow, with a man at the gate holding skulls 'apparently with the view of increasing the excitement of the persons assembled outside'. Over several months, an estimated 6,000 people came to view the vault. It was also described in detail by the press, often with an emphasis on its slum location: 'windings of narrow and dirty lanes . . . an obscure and choked up market . . . a gloomy and frowsy court was pointed out to us by squalid children playing round a stagnant puddle.'

Like the dances, the Enon Chapel viewings tapped into a Victorian taste for the macabre, as well as what became a fashion for 'slumming'. Slumming was a kind of urban tourism, the spirit of colonial exploration turned instead on the city's poor. From the mid nineteenth century, the wealthy and middle classes were becoming increasingly aware of conditions in the slums, often through the shocking reports of investigative journalists. At the time, Charles Dickens was also publishing his novels, in popular weekly and monthly instalments, with their themes of poverty and injustice. Prompted by such reports, the rich dressed down and hung out in the slums, to see for themselves 'how the other half lived'. Motivations were varied and no doubt complex: curiosity, voyeurism, philanthropy and Christian charity, as well as a more blatant kind of thrill-seeking through sex or other 'guilty pleasures'. It was this that Oscar Wilde drew on when he wrote of Dorian Gray's visits to Bluegate Fields: by the time the novel was published, groups of wealthy slummers were being taken out to the East End on popular midnight bus tours.

In the crawling Friday night traffic, my own bus had gone

no more than a hundred yards. Outside, the upper storeys of buildings slid by, as we drew level with 190 Strand and stopped. I could see nothing of the building site behind, just the tops of windows emblazoned with SOPHISTICATED LIVING and WORLD-CLASS ADDRESS.

My thoughts returned to my own family. In the summer of 1851 – a few months after her details were filled in on the census form – the Tolladays' two-year-old daughter, Jessie, caught measles and died five days later. On her death certificate, in the box titled 'present at the death', instead of a signature the registrar has written 'the mark of Ellen Tolladay', which is how I learned she couldn't write. At the end of the following summer, having been ill with consumption since early spring, Ellen also died. Consumption is the old name for tuberculosis, derived from the way the disease consumes its sufferers. For most, this meant a slow wasting away towards death. Soon after opening the death certificate, I realized that, at the time she died, two of Ellen's children were the same age as mine. I was undone by this, by a wave of recognition that swept away the time and generations between us. How would it feel to know I could no longer take care of my children, that I would be leaving them in a place like that?

After her death, the remaining family went on living at number 17. From everything I'd read about the street and its residents, I could only assume this was in the same room where Jessie and Ellen had died. Then two years later – within six weeks of each other – both William and his eldest daughter, Jane, died too. All four of the death certificates are written in the painstakingly neat hand of the same registrar, and state that all of them died at the house. William died of emphysema, a progressive lung disease exacerbated by smoking and air pollution, which he already had at the time of his wife's death. And like her mother, Jane died of tuberculosis, a contagious disease that can remain dormant in the body for years after initial infection, only emerging when the immune system weakens.

Sitting on the stationary bus, I kept returning to that room, to the family living so close together in a place where four of them would die. I'd read so much about death: about the slums and that street in particular, about the state of the graveyards, about families sharing a room with the body of a loved one as they tried to raise money for a burial.

I stared out at the gathering dark, as the bus juddered forwards and WORLD-CLASS ADDRESS slipped away behind us.

3

Bermondsey

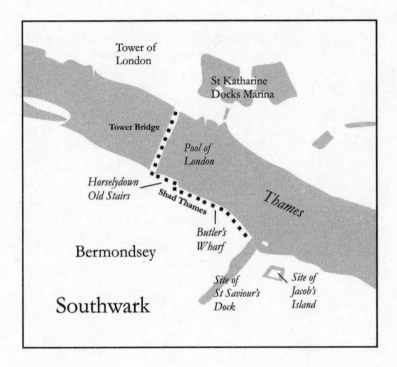

Tower of
London

St Katharine
Docks Marina

Tower Bridge

*Pool of
London*

*Horselydown
Old Stairs*

Shad Thames

Thames

*Butler's
Wharf*

Bermondsey

Southwark

*Site of
St Saviour's
Dock*

*Site of
Jacob's
Island*

Despite everything, four of the Tolladay children survived, although in the years following their parents' deaths I could find no trace of them. On an 1868 map – fourteen years after they were orphaned – Clements Lane and six acres of surrounding courts and alleyways have vanished. The area is blank and stamped 'SITE OF GROUND TO BE OCCUPIED BY THE NEW COURTS OF LAW'. In 1866, a *Times* columnist described the area as 'being fast deserted. Massive padlocks guard every door . . . By the displacement of so many hundreds of poor families . . . the unhealthy [neighbouring] courts, already reeking and noisome with excess of numbers, have become more overcrowded than ever.'

It was a common story. The St Giles rookeries had been pulled down to make way for New Oxford Street, with a knock-on worsening of conditions in neighbouring slums. The Victorian solution to the problem of slums was largely eviction and demolition, driving through large-scale civil-engineering projects to improve the flow of traffic, which was seen as necessary for continued economic growth. Wide new streets and triumphal buildings would also be a far more appropriate reflection of London's imperial and commercial status. And as the city grew and became wealthier, it needed somewhere to dump those things it didn't want – from its mountainous dustheaps and unwanted people to the most unpleasant of its industries.

A month after finding Water Street, I returned to London to trace that first stage of the Tolladays' migration from the city centre. I crossed the Thames at Tower Bridge early on a Sunday morning, surprised to find tourists already leaning out over the water with their phones on selfie sticks. On the south side, I took the steps down into Bermondsey and followed Shad Thames, a narrow cobbled street behind Victorian warehouses lining the river.

I'd come to Bermondsey because when I did find records of the surviving Tolladay children as adults, all four had left the slums of central London. Following the waves of migrant poor to London's expanding suburbs, the eldest had moved out to the East End and the other three were now spread across south London, all living close to the course of another of the city's lost rivers, the Neckinger. So I'd decided to go mudlarking on a stretch of the Bermondsey foreshore close to where the Neckinger joins the Thames. It was at nearby Leather Market that the youngest son, Robert − orphaned at the age of four − worked as a costermonger.

By then his brother, my great-great-grandfather Tom Tolladay, lived a mile away near the Elephant and Castle, off East Lane Market − the one that features in the title sequences of *Only Fools and Horses*. Before the Industrial Revolution, that part of Southwark was an area of marshy fields, common grazing and market gardens, with its name, Walworth, deriving from the Saxon 'Farm of the Britons'. As elsewhere in south London, much of the early development had been in ribbons along main roads leading out across marshes from the new Thames bridges.

Until the late 1700s, the main Walworth Road was lined with 'elegant mansions', but as industrialization gathered pace it brought rapid change to the suburbs. Not only was London's population growing at a spectacular rate, but areas closer to the city − like Bermondsey − were filling with factories and warehouses. The introduction of horse buses, trams and trains meant it was also becoming possible for people to live further from their place of work. Consecutive maps from the 1800s show Walworth's fields disappearing fast, as building speculators bought up the land. Side roads appear and fill with rows of terraced housing; and as the poor moved in, the wealthy moved out. Shops were built in the front gardens of the grand houses along Walworth Road and their upper storeys let and sublet to families. By the time Tom Tolladay lived there, the whole area was 'closely packed with streets of working-class houses'.

A description of individual streets can be found in Charles Booth's notebooks for his monumental *Inquiry into Life and Labour in London*. This study was the result of an investigation Booth began in 1886 amid growing concerns around social inequality. Industrialization may have brought wealth and rising living standards for many, but it was also increasing the numbers living in urban poverty. Booth himself was a wealthy shipowner, disillusioned with politics and religion, who began his investigation after disputing a claim that a quarter of London's population now lived in poverty. Setting out to show the true proportion was less than a quarter, instead – following an extraordinary eighteen-year investigation – he concluded that it was over a third. And while many of his researchers turned to socialism as a result of the appalling things they witnessed, the views of Booth himself became more strongly conservative. He warned that if the government did not act, it could lead to a socialist revolution.

One of the most striking elements of his study was the accompanying series of 'poverty maps', with each London street hand-coloured to show the relative income and social class of its inhabitants. These maps were compiled from notes written up by Booth's investigators, who accompanied local police on their beats. From these, Booth divided the population into seven colour-coded classes. These ranged from black ('Lowest class. Vicious, semi criminal') and dark blue ('Very poor, casual. Chronic want') to red ('Middle class. Well-to-do') and golden yellow ('Upper-middle and upper classes. Wealthy').

In Walworth, the streets where my family lived are coloured blue and listed simply as Poor. In the notebooks, East Lane Market is described as having 'third-rate shops on either side of the road' and being 'busiest on Sunday mornings when all shops are open and the place is filled with hawkers, quack doctors, all sorts'. In 1899, Tom Tolladay lived at Lestock Place. This was on Sergeant E. Wyatt's beat and on 30 June the researcher accompanying him described the local streets in a black notebook (a square of yellowed paper stuck to the front has the handwritten request: 'If found, Please return to Charles Booth, 9 Adelphi Terrace, Strand'). After a hand-drawn diagram of the sergeant's beat, the researcher has written of Lestock Place: 'rooms bare, many children, hatless, dirty, bad boots'. Next they walked down King and Queen Street: 'very poor costers . . . rough, many charges for drunkenness and assaults among themselves'. And from there they turned into Beddome Street – 'poor, doors open, general labourers' – which is where Tom's son, my scavenger great-grandfather, lived.

When I reached Horselydown Old Stairs the iron gates stood open. The stairs to the shore lead up and then down through a passageway in the old brewery building, and I stood at the top of the steps in the gloom. The lower flight was green with algae, and now and then the tea-coloured Thames sloshed up over the crumbling bottom tread. The tide was higher than I'd expected and it would be a while before I could get down on the shore.

So first I walked east along the river, keen to see the tidal inlet at the mouth of the Neckinger, which was once St Saviour's Dock. For the first stretch the riverside was dominated by the vast Butler's Wharf, now a complex of restaurants and luxury flats. In the nineteenth century it was reputed to be the largest tea warehouse in the world, at the centre of the Pool of London with its chaos of waiting ships and lighters. Unlike the south bank further west, the Bermondsey riverside has retained more of a feel of its past – and, that morning, of the night before as well: huge old anchors and propellers were set into walkways as sculpture, with beer bottles and plastic glasses stood carefully beneath them. More bottles were tucked in amongst the flowers in planters, and beneath the waterfront railings lay clusters of cigarette butts, a modern echo of all the discarded clay pipes. Outside Conran's Chop House a man lay on a strip of Astroturf facing the wall, fast asleep with his head wrapped in a jacket and his shoes placed carefully together at his side.

I stopped at the bridge across the inlet that was once St Saviour's Dock. Below, what remained of the Neckinger was draining away into the Thames, revealing a slick expanse of river-bottom mud. From medieval times, the history of Bermondsey has been shaped by its position at the confluence of the Thames and Neckinger. By the time it was recorded in the Domesday Book, Beormund's Eyot was already known as Bermundeseye: a 'gravel island' of grazing marsh and woodland surrounded by tidal saltmarsh. At its heart was the priory that became Bermondsey Abbey, and it was monks from there who dug the early drainage dykes and embankments to reclaim the low-lying marshland. At the mouth of the Neckinger they built the Mill of St Saviour and later, in the thirteenth century, the neighbouring St Saviour's Dock. In this area of cultivated pasture, orchards and market gardens, local place names included 'le waterweye' and 'le watergang' – thought to refer to those early tidal streams.

Increasingly, though, Bermondsey was also shaped by its proximity to the city. By the fourteenth century, the polluting and grim-smelling tanneries were already being banished from the centre and moving south across the river. Given the tanners' need for space and a plentiful supply of water, the mouth of the Neckinger and its tidal streams offered an ideal location.

Impatient to get down on the shore, I headed back to Horselydown Old Stairs (the name said to derive from the medieval 'Horsridune', meaning 'hill in the marsh where horses are kept', which by the fifteenth century had become 'Horse-lie-down'). I entered the gloomy passageway for a second time, passing a notice at the gates giving a mobile-phone number in case I returned to find them locked – as when the tide rises here, these stairs are the only way out.

The tunnel-like passage and low light intensified the separation between city and shore, and as the walls brightened I breathed the smell of the river. For just a moment it was clean like the sea, closely followed by familiar underlayers of mud, weed and decay. As is sometimes the case, though, on reaching the bottom of the stairs I was disappointed to find the retreating tide had left a slick layer of silt obscuring much of the shore. From past experience I knew that only the wake of the first boats would wash this away, but it was early and they had to pass before the tide fell too low.

Meanwhile, in the shadow of a looming Tower Bridge, I headed for the dark drift of the strandline at the top of the shore, which the fickle tide had left clear of mud. Like the sea, the river sorts its flotsam by density, so as usual there was a lot of damp bone and plastic; amongst it today was a modern shoe heel, the arm from a pair of glasses and several black cable ties.

Although I don't often take them home, first in the bag was a sculptural bone, almost the colour of wood. When I'd first wandered down onto the Thames foreshore twenty-five years earlier – never having heard of a mudlark – it was the animal bones that struck me most. They were something I rarely found on sea beaches, but here they seemed to be everywhere. It added to the early strangeness of being down on the foreshore in the middle of a city, not knowing if it was legal to be there, or what might be allowed. At the time, I also had no idea why the bones were there, imagining they must be waste from nearby restaurants.

Later, though, I learned that many date to the eighteenth and nineteenth centuries, from carcasses dumped in the river by slaughterhouses. And one reason so many are stained a dark colour was the appalling state of the Thames at the time. On previous visits I've found (but left behind) horns and vertebrae, fragments of skull, thighbones and ball-and-socket joints – many with the distinctive marks of a butcher's cleaver. There are also plenty of teeth: from sheep, cattle and pigs, as well as dogs. The horse teeth can be particularly striking, often a beautiful blue-grey, with some so big they must have come from dray horses (some lucky mudlarks have even found the teeth of woolly mammoths and straight-tusked elephants).

Amongst the stranded bones there were also scraps of leather, which blacken and stiffen between tides but never quite dry out – and one was from a hand-stitched shoe. Due to the wonderfully anaerobic Thames mud, over the years beautifully preserved medieval and Tudor shoes have been eased from its grip; even Roman sandals have survived more or less intact for close to 2,000 years. So there is always the chance that these scraps of hand-sewn leather might be ancient. Which is the reason that more than once I've arrived on the foreshore to find a modern shoe dug painstakingly from the mud and then left, disappointedly, in a heap. Unlike recent shoes, the remains from previous centuries are often studded with hobnails, which made the soles last longer, or show the marks of repeated re-heeling and re-soling. For, as with so much else, when shoes were handmade by a craftsman they were expensive to replace, so would usually be kept in use for as long as possible.

Perhaps with half a mind on tanneries, I picked up more

leather than usual. A couple of the pieces were straplike, again with irregular hand-stitched holes, and appeared to be from reins or a bridle. A few months earlier, I'd also picked up something that may well have been used by leather workers, and which has since become a favourite find. That day I was searching on the north bank of the Thames, glancing up from the foreshore now and then to see a woman making her way slowly along the waterline towards me. Wearing bright blue disposable gloves, she would stop every few yards to kneel and search a patch more closely. She worked methodically, entirely absorbed and intent, scraping at the mud with a trowel (stiff from crouching, I was envious of the squashy kneepads she wore). I gave her a wide berth as we passed, so as not to encroach on her patch – although I wasn't sure she even knew I was there. Looping back down to the water's edge, I felt faintly discouraged, knowing it had already been thoroughly searched. There was something in the quality of her attention that made it seem unlikely she'd miss anything good.

So I was surprised when only minutes later I spotted a metal band lying clearly on the surface. It was grey-brown, with slightly irregular divots, and so obvious I presumed she'd rejected it. Perhaps it was just a piece of machinery. As it was roughly the size of a finger, I slipped it on – to find it fitted perfectly. It narrowed slightly at the top, preventing it from sliding down to where a ring would sit. I slipped it off and on, off and on. Worn beautifully smooth on the inside, it seemed too good a fit not to have been made for a finger. I wondered if it might be a thimble that had lost its top. At the laptop later that evening, I searched for anything similar on the Portable Antiquities Scheme database (a wonderful resource run by the British Museum and National Museum Wales that records archaeological objects found by members of the public). There I found a thimble almost identical to mine. It turned out it never did have a top. Described as a medieval or early post-medieval 'ring-type thimble', it dated from 1450 to 1600, and on a later visit to the Finds Liaison Officer I learned that as well as being used to stitch cloth, thimbles of this type were also used by leatherworkers.

I was still crouching on the Bermondsey strandline when finally a boat passed, its wake washing away a great swathe of mud from the shore. A series of waves followed in quick succession, sloshing up over my boots and leaving just a strip of mud stranded high on shore. At least I could see the stones now. I dropped a second 'rein' in the bag, as although scraps of leather are common finds on the foreshore, some would date to the nineteenth century – by which time Bermondsey was known as the Land of Leather.

By then, tanneries clustered along its riverbanks and at the mouth of the Neckinger. The word 'tanning' is from the Latin for oak bark, which was added to the tanning pits until the advent of chemical tanning in the late 1800s. It is a slow and evil-smelling process, which in effect mummifies the hides to prevent them from rotting. At the tanneries, the fresh skins were first scraped, 'fleshed' and degreased, and then left in quicklime, or soaked in urine and kneaded with 'dung-water' made from dog faeces collected by the pure-finders. This soaking was done in open-air tanning pits and could take more than a year. By the mid 1800s, Bermondsey was home to more than a third of Britain's leather industry, with a single one of its tanneries processing 45,000 bullock hides and 10,000 horse hides a year. At the nearby Neckinger Mill, annual production was half a million of the softer, more expensive skins such as deer, kid and seal. Twice a day, Bermondsey's network of tidal ditches flushed a vast area of tanning pits, sweeping the waste away into the Thames. In a piece Henry Mayhew wrote for the *Morning Chronicle* in 1849, he described those ditches: 'In some parts the fluid is almost as red as blood from the colouring matter that pours into it from the reeking leather-dressers close by.'

Inevitably, Bermondsey's concentration of tanneries drew

related industries to the area. These included end users of the leather trade such as shoemakers and upholsterers, the saddle and harness trade, and luggage- and hatmakers, as well as those who could make use of the tanners' waste. Soap boilers and candlemakers would take 'wet' bones to boil off the fat (there were rumours that south London's tallowmakers also bought bones from the grave robbers). Cat-gut cleaners bought the intestines of sheep and goats to make strings for harps and violins, and gluemakers could make use of almost any remains. As well as bones, they took the damaged pelts and fleshings, the 'sloughs' from cattle horn, and waste scraps from the neighbouring trotter boilers, dressers and furriers.

Being outside the regulation and restrictions of the City, Bermondsey also attracted other polluting industry to its riverbanks and tidal ditches, from paper mills, breweries and dyers to jam and soap factories. By the mid nineteenth century, St Saviour's Mill – originally a watermill built by the monks to grind flour – was a coal-powered lead mill, with the tanners' spent bark used to turn grey lead white for skin-lightening face paints and enamels. It was just one of a vast number of coal-fired factories that now spewed as much pollution into the air as into the Thames, regularly shrouding the city in soot-drenched smogs, which were often worst in these low-lying areas by the river.

I was hunkered down at the water's edge when voices echoed in the passageway behind me. I glanced around to see a couple in wedding clothes emerge with a photographer: the first people I'd seen since I arrived. The photographer led them down onto the shore, directing in what sounded like Russian, gesturing towards the river and Tower Bridge. Holding on to her partner's arm, the woman picked her way across the stones in high heels. She stopped just short of the glistening layer of silt. White flowers were fixed in her hair and her bright blue dress flared out at the waist – from where I was, she looked incongruously clean against a backdrop of weed and rotting wood. Reluctantly, I edged away from what seemed a good spot, aware that no one wants their wedding photographs to include a stranger squatting in the mud.

Soon afterwards, at a spot more obviously out of shot, I picked up an old fly button and a couple of coins. As often, the first turned out to be no more than a corroded two-pence piece, but the second was better: a 1942 farthing with the image of a wren. Later, while researching Jacob's Island – a notorious slum that grew up nearby at the mouth of the Neckinger – I learned that its squalid lanes and passageways included a Farthing Alley.

Jacob's Island epitomized how Victorian London's appalling slum conditions were exacerbated by the vast amount of waste the city now produced. As well as the human and animal waste the Thames had carried away since medieval times, by the mid nineteenth century its dark, sluggish waters were contaminated with everything from toxic industrial effluent to waterborne diseases such as dysentery, typhoid and cholera. And at Jacob's Island, the poorest lived amongst its reeking tidal ditches.

In *Oliver Twist*, Charles Dickens used the area as the last grim refuge for the vicious criminal Bill Sikes. Dickens knew Jacob's Island from visits with the river police, describing it in the novel as

> the filthiest, the strangest, the most extraordinary of the many localities that are hidden in London . . . Crazy wood galleries common to the backs of half-a-dozen houses, with holes from which to look upon the slime beneath; windows, broken and patched, with poles thrust out, on which to dry the linen that is never there; rooms so small, so filthy, so confined, that the air would seem too tainted even for the dirt and squalor which they shelter; wooden chambers thrusting themselves out above the mud, and threatening to fall into it, as some have done;

dirt-besmeared walls and decaying foundations; every repulsive lineament of poverty, every loathsome indication of filth, rot, and garbage.

In 1849 Henry Mayhew also visited Jacob's Island for the *Morning Chronicle*, describing it as 'the Venice of Drains'. This was at the height of a cholera epidemic, exacerbated by the 1847 law requiring toilets to be connected to mains sewers, which in turn fed into the river. Trapped by the tides, the raw sewage now pouring into the Thames simply sloshed back and forth twice a day. On Jacob's Island, toilets were anyway little more than 'open doorless privies that hang over the water side' which – like the industrial waste from nearby factories and tanneries – simply emptied straight into the river.

The water is covered with a scum almost like a cobweb, and prismatic with grease . . . As we passed along the reeking banks of the sewer the sun shone upon a narrow slip of the water. In the bright light it appeared the colour of strong green tea, and positively looked as solid as black marble in the shadow – indeed it was more like watery mud than muddy water; and yet we were assured this was the only water the wretched inhabitants had to drink.

It was in the subsequent 1854 epidemic that Dr John Snow, sceptical of the dominant miasma theory, first demonstrated that cholera was waterborne. Yet it would be another thirty years before the authorities accepted this (with some feeling that the 'faecal-oral' nature of transmission might prove too unpleasant for the public to contemplate).

Despite water companies continuing to draw their water from the Thames, by the following year that particular cholera epidemic had run its course, and little changed. Raw sewage and industrial waste continued to pour into the Thames and its tributaries. It wasn't until 1858 – during one of the hottest summers on record – that the appalling state of the river finally became a more pressing concern for the rich and powerful.

As temperatures continued to rise, *The Times* claimed Londoners were now unwilling to travel on the river, 'afraid not only of prospective disease, but of immediate nausea, headache and giddiness'. Amid growing pressure from the press, another *Times* editorial protested, 'They are now doing nothing but throwing a few boatloads of lime into the river.'

With the Houses of Parliament situated on the banks of the Thames, politicians soon found themselves at the centre of what became known as the Great Stink. As the Palace of Westminster's riverside rooms filled with the stench of sewage, MPs complained of having a choice between being 'half choked and half poisoned by the disgusting smell if the windows are kept open' and 'literally baked' if they were closed. Meanwhile, the palace's curtains were soaked in bleach in an effort to disguise the smell. Parliamentary sittings were abandoned and by the height of summer, government could barely function. 'Is it possible', asked one MP, 'that the Parliament can any longer sit in London if the Thames is not purified?'

Why waste time with parliamentary meetings, asked the *Era* newspaper, when 'everyone knew that the plan was to take the sewage out of London to Kent or Essex'? Although the scale of the problem was vast, a bill was passed that July in a record eighteen days. In his address to Parliament, Prime Minister Benjamin Disraeli described the state of the Thames:

> That noble river, so long the pride and joy of Englishmen, which has hitherto been associated with the noblest feats of our commerce and the most beautiful passages of our poetry, has really become a Stygian pool, reeking with ineffable and intolerable horrors.

The outcome was Joseph Bazalgette's ambitious system of sewers, opened in 1865 and completed a decade later. It was a feat of Victorian engineering that incorporated some of the city's lost rivers and ran beneath the vast new embankments (reclaiming twenty-two acres of land from the Thames, and dismaying the mudlarks). In narrowing the Thames through the city centre, it was also hoped that the strengthened flow would sweep other pollution downstream, rather than leaving it trapped in London by the tides. Unfortunately, the sewage discharged downriver did not flow out with the tides as hoped; instead great 'mud-banks' built up around the outlets. With this new 'away' proving to be not quite far enough away, by the 1890s London had 'a fleet of fine sludge ships'. Known as the 'Bovril boats', these carried the city's separated 'solid sewage' out to Black Deep off the Essex coast to be dumped at sea.

It was midmorning when I heard again the echo of voices from the passageway above the stairs. By then I'd been on the foreshore for a couple of hours and although occasionally someone had come briefly down onto the stones, on the whole I'd been by myself. Turning round, I was surprised to see another photographer directing a couple in wedding clothes. This time they all spoke Chinese and the bride walked out onto the foreshore in a brilliant white dress. Unlikely as it seemed from out there in the mud, I appeared to have stumbled on a popular location for the iconic Tower Bridge wedding shot. So once again I moved out of the way.

The appalling state of the Thames in Victorian times did of course also have a devastating effect on the natural life of the river, where once watermen had complained of their oars becoming entangled in waterlilies. A major casualty was the once-plentiful eel, a staple food of working-class Londoners for centuries – no doubt including all those generations of my own family.

A few days earlier I'd found my first on the shore. It was no longer alive, but lay on the wet stones in a gentle curve, as if pausing in its journey down to the water. (One of the many extraordinary things about eels is that they're able to travel across land, due to a coating of slime and the ability to absorb oxygen through their skin.)

In a pre-refrigeration era, when most meat and fish had to be preserved in salt, eels could be kept alive in no more than a tray or puddle of water. And as London's population exploded, they became an increasingly popular street food, with the mid nineteenth century also seeing the first pie and mash shops selling eels in green 'liquor'. Writing in 1854, the Reverend David Badham described the city and its eels:

> London steams and teems with eels alive and stewed. For one halfpenny, a man of the million may fill his stomach with six or seven long pieces and wash them down with a sip of the glutinous liquid they are stewed in.

In the past, my mum had mentioned the eels at East Lane Market, so back home in Cornwall I phoned her to ask more about them. (We both speak with the same cockney–estuary lack of clear pronunciation and there is nothing wrong with her hearing.)

'Mum,' I said when she answered, 'can I come round and ask you about eels?'

'Ills?'

'Eels.'

'Ills?'

'EELS.'

She raised her voice too. 'ILLS?'

Neither of us had any idea what the other was saying. (It turned out one of her responses was 'hills', one was 'eels' and another wondered if I was asking about hers and my dad's health.)

'Eels, Mum. 'E. E. L. S.'

'Oh, eels. Yes, course you can.'

So I drove the few miles to her house and she was soon

telling me that when she was little, her mum – my Nan Tolladay – went shopping 'down the lane' three days a week. Eels were bought from the fishmonger's stall, where they were kept alive in metal trays out the back.

'You never bought a dead eel,' she said.

So while my nan browsed at the front of the fishmonger's stall – 'she took ages and it was boring' – my mum would sneak around the back to touch them. On the days my nan did choose eels, the fishmonger would pick them up with newspaper and chop off the heads, and my nan would carry them home, still wriggling, in her shopping bag.

They were not nearly as popular on the Isle of Sheppey, where we lived from the 1970s, so to buy jellied eels you had to drive out to where the holidaying Londoners stayed: to the caravan sites at the far end of the island. Personally, I never took to jellied eels, but I remember as a child watching various family members uneasily as they wolfed down the chunks with relish – grey skin, cold jelly and all – and then fished around in their mouths for bones.

At that point my dad came in and said his islander mum wouldn't have eels in the house because they looked like snakes. So if he caught them out fishing he'd throw them back – until the time he and a friend caught twenty-five out on the marshes and brought them back for Nan Tolladay to stew (by then she and my grandad had moved to the island as well). Back home in the kitchen, he couldn't hold them still to cut off the heads.

'It was a bloodbath,' he said. 'Eels were climbing up out of the sink with no heads.'

He shuddered. 'There was blood all up the walls. Even the chopped-up bits kept on moving.'

After that, any eels he caught were always thrown back.

From its colour and small size, the washed-up eel I found on the shore that day was an elver. The name is said to have evolved from the annual 'eel fare' or 'eel fair' – with fare meaning travel and referring to the annual mass migration of young eels up the Thames. With the young eels still entering the estuary in large numbers in Victorian times, the naturalist C. J. Cornish described how 'they made a black margin to the river, on either side of the banks'. These writhing masses of juvenile eels were easy pickings and people flocked to the river, rolling up their trousers and wading in with nets and buckets or whatever was to hand.

Eels had always been plentiful in the Thames. From Roman times they had been hooked and speared, caught in pots, nets and traps, and for centuries baited with worms woven into balls of worsted wool. Yet until the 1920s, no one knew where the young eels came from. For over 2,000 years, philosophers and scientists had been speculating on the mystery of their reproduction; in Ancient Greece, Aristotle proposed that they were born of earthworms and grew from the 'guts of wet soil'. Four hundred years later, in first-century Rome, Pliny the Elder believed that eels reproduced by rubbing their bodies against rocks and that 'from the shreds of skin thus detached come new ones'. Later, other wild theories abounded: they were born from their own slime, from the anus of a particular beetle, from the action of sunlight on dew. One bishop told the Royal Society that young eels 'slithered from the roofs of thatched cottages'.

First published by the Danish scientist Johannes Schmidt in 1922, the true story of eel reproduction turned out to be every bit as extraordinary as the earlier theories. Following a backwards trail of ever-smaller eel larvae, Schmidt eventually arrived at the Sargasso Sea. Today, it is widely known that every eel – in every one of our rivers, inland ponds and muddy ditches – began life some 3,000 miles away in this legendary sea around Bermuda, with its reputation as a graveyard of ships. In *The Book of Eels*, Tom Fort writes that each eel is 'born of an egg in a sac of oil suspended above the prodigious depth of the strangest sea on earth'. Like the eye of a hurricane, the Sargasso is at the centre of a circular 'gyre' created by the convergence of five ocean currents, and takes its name from the mats of Sargassum weed seen floating at the surface. (After European sailors first crossed it in the fifteenth century, tales spread of wrecked and abandoned ships found trapped by the weed and lack of wind.) For whatever evolutionary reasons – perhaps oceanic and continental upheavals – every European eel is only able to spawn if it returns to that distant sea.

Once freed from the Sargasso's circular currents, the eel larvae drift towards Europe, carried by the Gulf Stream on a journey that can take anything from one to three years. While some remain at the coast or in estuaries, others enter rivers on the flood tide and are drawn upstream. On the ebb, the young 'glass eels' hug the riverbanks, where the seaward current is weakest (making them easy prey during the eel fares). The changing salinity then triggers their transformation into elvers, like the one I found, and for the next ten to fifteen years – occasionally thirty or forty – the mature eels are elusive, hunting mainly at night and spending the winters fasting in mud-holes. Incredibly, the only way they are able to reproduce is to return to the Sargasso Sea. No one is quite sure what triggers this epic migration, but one autumn the eel's muscled body begins to turn silver; it also stops feeding and the gut degenerates, as it will make the 3,000-mile journey on stored energy alone (silver eels are not caught at sea because they don't take bait). Often on a moonless night after heavy rain, the eels leave the security of the mud banks to begin their gruelling journey back across the Atlantic Ocean. In the past this exodus would be on a staggering scale, and people told of seeing masses of eels writhing through wet grass to reach streams and rivers. Exactly how they find their way back remains a mystery, although recent research suggests that they use the earth's magnetic fields to locate the Gulf Stream, and can then ride its warm currents back to the Sargasso Sea.

In Victorian London though, the Thames eels were in trouble, from both pollution and over-consumption. Eaten in such vast quantities by the city's burgeoning population, they were also shipped in from overseas. The Dutch eel *schuyts* in particular were some of the Thames's most curious craft: great broad-beamed 'floating sieves' that let water in to refresh their eel tanks. Granted tax privileges at Billingsgate from 1699 – in recognition of their help feeding Londoners after the Great Fire of 1666 – by the nineteenth century the *schuyts* had to moor downriver, due to the effects of pollution on the eels.

By the Great Stink of 1858, the state of the river was so bad that the *schuyts* were no longer able to moor anywhere close to the city centre: the influx of polluted Thames water was killing the imported Dutch eels in their holding tanks, forcing the *schuyts* to moor ever further downstream. Until the opening of Bazalgette's sewers in 1865, the raw sewage in particular was a disaster for the river's entire fish population, as the bacteria that break down effluent use up oxygen dissolved in water. With such vast quantities of sewage entering the Thames, this left too little for the fish to survive.

Subsequent decades saw dramatic improvements as a result of the new Victorian sewage system, but during the Second World War this was badly damaged by bombing. Once again raw sewage poured into the Thames and by 1957 – almost exactly a century after the Great Stink – a twelve-mile stretch of the river was declared 'biologically dead'. The eels had gone. And as every eel upstream has to migrate through central London in order to spawn, this affected populations in count-less tributaries, brooks and village ponds.

In more recent decades, stricter environmental controls have reduced the amount of industrial effluent, pesticides and fertilizers entering the river and water quality has improved dramatically. Yet despite notable successes – there are now 125 species of fish in the Thames as well as occasional porpoises, seals and even seahorses – something drastic is happening to the eels. In a pattern replicated across Europe, in recent years the Thames eel population has fallen to less than 5 per cent of levels in the 1980s. So while it might be less charismatic than giant pandas and polar bears, the once-abundant European eel is now classified alongside them as critically endangered and at risk of extinction.

Although scientists can't be sure of the reason behind such dramatic losses, a combination of factors is thought to be involved, many of which affect the eels' ability to undertake their epic migration. These range from man-made obstructions such as weirs and flood defences to illegal fishing and an introduced parasite affecting their swim bladders. Another possibility is that the changing climate and warming seas are altering ocean currents – in particular the Gulf Stream – affecting both the larvae arriving in Europe and the silver eels returning to spawn. With the Sargasso Sea as vast as it is, if eel numbers fall too low, those that do make it back may be unable to find a mate.

Research into yet another threat came about on the Thames by chance. During conservation tests using fyke nets – traditional eel traps anchored to riverbeds – researchers found that rather than catching eels and mitten crabs as intended, their nets kept filling with plastic. It turned out this wasn't just floating at the river's surface, but that a vast amount of hidden, submerged plastic was also making its way slowly along the riverbed and out to sea. As many of us are only just beginning to realize, we are replicating the same old pattern that devastated the Thames in Victorian times: pollute now and (perhaps) clean up later.

After a glance through the day's meagre finds, I made my way back up the weed-furred steps to the tunnel leading back to

Combs: bone and plastic, seventeenth–twenty-first century. The fine side
of the bone combs was used to tease out nits. Eighty-two similar combs
were found on the *Mary Rose* – a Tudor warship that sank in 1545 and
was raised in the 1980s – with several still containing nits that were
almost five hundred years old.

Kelp with a golf ball as its anchor rock.

Kitchen cupboard, with some favourite shore finds.

Coral and a money cowrie. Neither species is native to Britain, but both turn up in the Thames as they were used as ballast on merchant sailing ships. Money cowries were also shipped on to Africa for use as payment in the slave trade.

Pink sea fan skeletons with nylon net, rope and fishing line. The dense, twig-like remains of these horny corals sink to the sea floor and become entangled with debris. They often wash ashore in Cornwall after gales.

Pink sea fan with washing instructions.

Cabinet of finds, including a parachute man, the
jawbones of a sea urchin and a teddy's eye.

Buttons and beads made from bone, metal, mother-of-pearl, glass and plastic, seventeenth–twenty-first century, along with the waste from making bone buttons or beads by hand – each half-circle shows the space where a disc was removed.

Smoking-related shore finds, seventeenth–twenty-first century: clay pipe bowls, plastic cigar tips and modern cigarette filters. The smallest clay pipes are the oldest, dating from the 1600s, with the size of the bowls increasing as the price of tobacco fell.

Lid from a silver sugar bowl, twentieth century.

Lead horse's head: a nineteenth-century child's toy,
found on the Isle of Sheppey.

Teaspoons, nineteenth–twentieth century. Originally an apothecary's measure – a fluid drachm – the teaspoon grew in size in the eighteenth century (from a quarter of a tablespoon to a third) as tea and sugar became less expensive.

Plastic cherry.

Lead and aluminium tube-mouths, probably from
toothpaste tubes, nineteenth–twentieth century.

Shore finds, seventeenth–twenty-first century, including a pewter blow-hole button (1650–1750), a roll-on deodorant ball, plastic cap-gun ammunition, a brass tap, Pop-it beads, a lid from a silver sugar bowl, a Codd marble (1870s–1920s), a castor wheel, a bayonet light-bulb fitting, an escutcheon and nurdles.

Beach finds, mainly twentieth century, including a snake belt buckle, a toggle light switch, a wren farthing (1937–56), a fly button, a zip pull, a model propeller, a death's head button (single hole), a curtain runner, a safety pin and a police shoulder number.

'Ring-type' thimble, 1450–1600, found on the Thames foreshore in central London. Thimbles of this kind were used by tailors and leatherworkers.

Toothbrushes: bone, vintage plastic and modern combination plastics, nineteenth–twenty-first century.

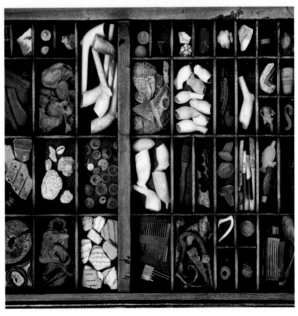

Mudlarking finds: Roman and medieval to present day.

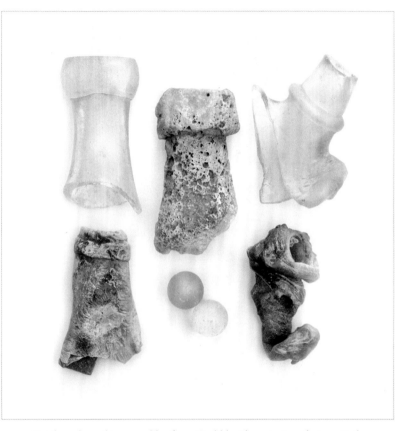

Bottlenecks and two marbles from Codd bottles, nineteenth–twentieth century. Found at Bottle Beach on the Swale marshes amongst the remains of London's barged-out rubbish, most of them heat damaged.

Crotal bell found on the Isle of Sheppey, seventeenth–eighteenth century. Also known as rumble bells, these were often attached to horses' harnesses to warn of approaching horse-drawn vehicles. Although damaged, this one still has the pea inside.

the street. Sixty years ago – the year the Thames was declared biologically dead – my mum was at school a ten-minute walk from here. The building stood between a glue factory, a soap factory and a tannery, and the main thing I recall her saying is that everyone always kept the windows shut – except the French teacher, who would shout '*Ouvrez la fenêtre!*' until someone opened a window and the whole place stank.

Until then, for three generations the Tolladays had gone on living within a few streets of East Lane Market. In that time, as people continued flocking from the countryside to the city, London's population had exploded. At 1 million in 1800, a century later it was approaching 7 million. As the city sprawled ever further from the centre, my mum's generation was the first to leave Walworth. In time, like so many others, all four siblings again moved further out – with my own family continuing our eel-like migration downriver to the sea. Our next stop – for two decades – was the Isle of Sheppey in the Thames Estuary, and it was on beaches there that I first learned that similar journeys were made by London's refuse.

For, once the great suburban dust-heap had become unacceptable, mountains of the stuff needed dumping further afield.

PART II

The Estuary

4

Bottle Beach

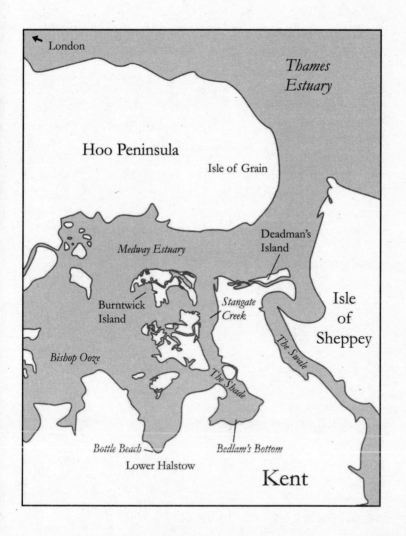

I was woken early by the first passing cars. My van was parked on an old friend's driveway beside a main road, and up in the canvas roof it was like waking in a tent on the pavement. I climbed down, foot-first on the shoulder of the driver's seat, and put the kettle on. Within minutes the windows had steamed up, drawing a veil over the rows of suburban houses and parked cars.

I'd spent the night there so I could catch the early tide. I was headed for one of many places around the Thames Estuary where landfill and dumping has artificially raised low-lying ground. For centuries Londoners' waste has left the city by barge, so these sites are often close to the water. Yet that leaves them at risk of erosion and, when high tides scour the river-banks, they expose refuse that's been buried for decades or centuries. I'd chosen a site out on Kent's Swale marshes, near the Isle of Sheppey, as it was used to dump the city's barged-out waste at the turn of the last century.

After packing down the van, I set off towards the estuary. The Swale marshes lie at the confluence of the Thames and Medway rivers, with their sixteenth-century name meaning 'a marshy depression'. The landscape was familiar from my childhood, with much of the wide-open grazing reclaimed from tidal saltmarsh. These areas were known as 'inned marshes' and, rather than fences, the fields are separated by ancient fleet and ditch systems, with their seaward limit protected by flood walls. Originally built from watertight 'puddled clay' – dug from nearby borrow dykes – in places the medieval sea walls are still 'fossilized' inside later defences. Usually, though, like the buried waterfronts in central London, the earlier walls are further inland, marking the progressive stages of land reclamation. Like much of the Thames Estuary, the Swale marshes have a long history of loss and gain, with the low-lying land always at risk of inundation. Since late medieval times, each century has recorded North Sea storm surges breaching sea walls and causing devastating floods here, with eyewitness accounts describing these surges as preceded by an unnatural low tide, which goes out further and for longer than expected.

I followed the marsh road out to the edge of the estuary, beyond the sea walls to the natural landscape of mudflats and tidal saltmarsh, its creeks and runnels filling and emptying with the tide. Offshore a string of marsh islands lay out at the horizon, so low they could barely be seen, and long since abandoned to the sea.

By the late nineteenth century, an increasing amount of London's rubbish was heading downriver to the marshes, as local authorities sought new ways of dealing with growing volumes of waste. Londoners now produced so much that the old methods of sorting and recycling were becoming impractical and uneconomic. It wasn't long after Henry Mayhew's visit to a London dustyard in the mid nineteenth century that the market for 'dust' had begun to collapse – industry's shift towards mechanization had made it easier and cheaper for producers to source virgin raw materials rather than recycled, and combined with rising wages this meant that many of the old, established markets for salvaged waste were drying up.

Just as important was a change in the way fossil fuels were now used in the home, with a shift away from using coal to gas. As a result the bulk of household waste was no longer valuable ash, which left the rest barely worth sorting. Without profits to be made from recycling, private waste contractors were becoming increasingly expensive. So by the 1880s, responsibility for London's waste was falling to parish authorities.

For a time there was a move towards huge, high-temperature incinerators known as 'dust destructors'. Coinciding with the first crematoriums, this technological and 'sanitary' solution suited the Victorian age, as fire was considered a great purifier. Some of the destructors also produced electricity: the inscription on the Hoxton plant, for example, read 'E PULVERE LUX ET VIS', meaning 'From dust, light and power'. But they produced foul-smelling emissions, making them unpopular with people living nearby, and it was also cheaper to simply barge the waste out of London. As one London County Council official said of the refuse, 'The natural solution is to shoot it in some sparsely inhabited district, where public opinion is not strong enough to effectually resent it being deposited.'

The estuary marshes were an obvious choice.

I pulled over in a layby at the wide-open sweep of Bedlam's Bottom. It wasn't yet 6 a.m. and the tide was still too high to find much on the beach where I was headed, so I made coffee and carried it out to the water. Without a breath of wind, there was no movement at all in the pale summer verges. Beyond them, although the tide had turned, the shallow basin was almost brim-full. For the first time in ages I breathed the smell of the edge of the marsh: of salt, mud and decay; of blackened, waterlogged stems.

Somewhere out on the marsh road a motorcycle backfired and I became aware of the faint background hum of traffic. There is an odd feel to these marshes, at once wild and remote, yet surrounded by a rim of distant industry. In the early light this was a delicate blue: the ephemeral shapes of dockside cranes, wind turbines that barely turned, a tracery of sagging power lines. Several miles away, the tower of the Kingsnorth Power Station was bathed in a rosy flush.

On the far side of the basin, the mirror surface of the water was broken by a stern-post and several blackened ribs – like a local echo of the Sargasso Sea, Bedlam's Bottom is a well-known graveyard of barge wrecks. This dead-end basin floods from the Shade, a narrow channel off Stangate Creek, and it's through there that the barges were towed at the end of their useful lives. Here they were 'laid out on the marsh': left at the muddy edge and deliberately sunk. Given the height of the morning's tide, few were visible now. Yet on maritime charts, the whole of Bedlam's Bottom is ringed with symbols warning of hazardous sunken vessels, with several places stamped 'Numerous Wrecks'.

Some of the hulked barges were once owned by Eastwood's, a local brickworks company, as they were used to transport the bricks up to London. And rather than make the return journey empty, they carried the city's refuse, or 'rough stuff', back to the marshes. This was a notoriously unpleasant cargo, especially in summer when the barges would be accompanied by swarms of flies. It could also be dangerous, with the twin risks of spontaneous combustion and carbon dioxide fumes. As a warning, the crew would keep a lamp alight in the cabin, and when lack of oxygen made the flame burn low, they headed out on deck.

Despite the grim nature of the cargo, by the mid 1800s there was fierce competition to handle these return freights, with barges often 'racing for a turn'. This is thought to be the origin of the first Thames Barge Match (the world's second oldest sailing race), which was started by the dust contractor Henry Dodd – believed to be the inspiration behind Charles Dickens's wealthy 'Golden Dustman' in *Our Mutual Friend*. Dodd was from a poor family and claimed to have worked previously as a scavenger at a London dustyard. Later he became a dust contractor, although it was the move to transporting the refuse by barge that made his fortune. He first hired and then invested in a fleet of Thames barges, and later bought several of the brickworks companies. By the 1870s, this self-made dust contractor was one of Britain's richest commoners. When he died in 1881, his estate included a Jacobean manor house and over £111,000: the equivalent of a 7-million-pound fortune today.

I stood with my tin mug of coffee watching the aerial dance of flies and mosquitoes, their gauzy wings backlit against the dark of stagnant pools. One of the reasons few people lived out on the marshes – making them an ideal dumping ground – was their unhealthy reputation, which we now know was due to the mosquitoes. Those who did live there were at risk of what were known as agues or 'marsh fevers', but was actually malaria. Like 'miasma', the word has its origins in the notion of 'bad air', with seventeenth-century visitors describing 'noxious vapours arising from the marshes subjecting the inhabitants to continued agues'.

Over the centuries, the Swale marshes have been a dumping ground not just for London's waste, but also its unwanted people. In particular, the sheltered waters of Stangate Creek provided ideal conditions to moor everything from quarantined 'plague ships' to floating prison hulks. Following the Great Plague of 1665, the creek became the main quarantine station for London-bound ships, initially against European outbreaks of plague and later for crews infected with yellow fever, smallpox and cholera. Disease was also rife on the prison hulks – decommissioned naval warships crudely converted to ease London's overcrowded prisons – and the moored prisoner-of-war ships, which held French soldiers captured during the Napoleonic Wars. Cramped and insanitary living conditions meant epidemics spread quickly and death rates could be high. As with London's overcrowded cemeteries, this brought the pressing problem of disposal of the dead.

Out here on the marshes, the solution was Deadman's Island. This lies close to the Isle of Sheppey and I knew of it as a child because my dad sometimes fished off it, in his boat with the distinctive-sounding engine that had come from a dumper truck. On this tiny island, the dead from Stangate Creek were buried in unmarked graves. And although at the time, the graves were dug close to the regulatory depth of six feet, today – due to the combination of rising sea levels and the sinking of south-east England – those coffins and bones are now emerging from the mud.

Owned by Natural England, the low-lying island is an important nesting site for wetland birds so landing is forbidden – and I've only seen it in photographs and films. The images can be both eerie and shocking. Like so much of the marsh, the island's low clay cliffs, no more than six feet high, are regularly scoured by the estuary tides. Below them, in the most disturbing images, the distinctive shapes of broken-open coffins protrude from the glistening clay. Human bones lie on the surface of the mud or in drifts of cockleshells: a jawbone, the curve of a pelvis, a thigh bone so long-exposed that it's studded with barnacles.

Deadman's Island lies out by the main shipping channel, where the currents are stronger. Given the increase in storms and surges that will come with climate change, rates of erosion are predicted to rise all along the Thames Estuary. Which means our hidden past will go on resurfacing, in what the writer Robert Macfarlane describes as untimely 'Anthropocene unburyings'. Along with so much else we thought we'd got rid of on these marshes, over coming decades that tiny island will go on giving up the bones of what are thought to be hundreds more bodies.

Half an hour later, I drove into the village of Lower Halstow and followed a tidy cul-de-sac to the edge of the marsh. From there, the path to the shore leads out through what is now a nature reserve, still known as the Brickfields despite their closure in 1966. In the half-century since then, scrubby tangles of hawthorn and bramble have overgrown any traces of industry, and at the end of the creek, the tiny dock stood empty.

The shore below is known locally as Bottle Beach (one of many Bottle Beaches on the estuary marshes), as it is strewn with the remains of pottery and glass brought down with the barged-out rubbish. I trod out across broken fragments littering the top of the shore: floral plates and cup handles, bottlenecks and the rims of jars, half a spout from a sturdy teapot – the scattered contents of Londoners' bins.

Having been carted away by the dustmen, the refuse was then barged out of the city as either 'rough stuff' – unsorted household waste – or partially sorted 'forked rough', of greater value as it contained more ash. If unsorted, it was unloaded at the creek-side wharves and dumped in fetid mounds around the brickfields. These would often be left for a year or more, allowing the organic waste to rot away or be eaten by birds and rats. Only then was the heap ready for the sorters, whose work was known locally as 'scrying' (thought to be a corruption of *descry*, meaning 'to discover by careful looking'). In theory, at least, the profit from any finds was the sorter's to keep, with a local rag-and-bone man making regular visits to the site.

As at the London dustyards, what remained after scrying was then 'riddled through', with the sifters separating the ash by banging metal sieves against their aproned bodies (by the 1900s, they also used a hand-turned machine). The fine ash passing through was then mixed with the clay to make bricks, while the coarser breeze was used as slow-burning fuel for the kilns. Much of the remaining hardcore – mainly crockery and glass – would then be dumped around the site. It was used to fill holes where the brick earth had been dug and lies beneath many of the more unnatural-looking hills surrounding disused brickfields. Here on the marshes it was also used to shore up floodwalls and raise low-lying ground, in ongoing efforts to reclaim land from the sea.

I crunched my way down the shore over the last of the rough stuff. After more than a century on the marshes, these tide-washed crocks were a world away from the grim heaps brought down on the barges – yet they still held clues to how habits were changing around the turn of the last century, along with the roots of our own wasteful ways.

Down at the muddy water's edge, one of the first things I lifted was a heavy bottle. It was almost whole and, as I looked it over, silty water streamed from the trailing wrack. The thick old glass was black and opaque, the bulging neck a little off-kilter. It was the kind of bottle used to carry wine from the cask to the table, and much of its weight was in the arched 'kick-up' at the base (familiar from wine bottles today, and reminding me of the old expression for someone drunk on wine: 'He drank until he saw the island'). It looked much older than other bottles here, which is not uncommon at Victorian dumps. Until the mid nineteenth century, containers were generally strong and built to last, in forms that were easy to clean, refill and reuse. A pre-Victorian bottle was thrown away because it had broken, not because it was empty (even then, attempts at repairing china and glass included metal rivets, homemade pastes made from tree sap, garlic and cheese, and tying it up and boiling it in milk). In dumps that can be closely dated, archaeologists have found glass bottles that appear to have been reused for more than a century.

As was evident on the lower shore, Victorian households also owned an array of utilitarian ceramic bowls and jars. Until the late nineteenth century, rather than being bought readymade, most products were mixed up at home from stores of raw ingredients. People had recipes for everything, from sauces and shoe blacking to egg-white hair cream and shampoos made from ammonia and 'old rum'. They shopped locally, with much of the food weighed out and wrapped in paper, and for things like ale, milk and cream they would take along their own jugs from home. Apart from organic remains such as scraps and bones, the average early Victorian bin contained little waste from the production of food.

By midmorning the bag was heavy. I'd barely noticed the tide slip away, yet slick mudflats now stretched off to the horizon, with the last of the draining creek no more than a distant ribbon of sky-shine. Out beyond the rotting ribs of hulked barges, a group of moored yachts now lay at drunken angles on the mud.

On the foreshore, the once-buoyant weed had collapsed around the bottles that anchored it, disguising their shapes. So I rooted about, washing the bottles in pools to look more closely at details, as the older glass has some wonderful clues to how it was produced. Like other dumps of a similar age, this beach usually turned up good examples of how bottle-making – like so many other industries – began the move away from hand-made techniques.

Rinsed clean, my favourite bottles so far were a delicate aqua. Although most of them weren't whole, their appeal lay in the hand-blown mistakes and irregularities: the asymmetry and uneven thicknesses, the air bubbles trapped inside the glass (depending on size, these are known by collectors as seeds or blisters). Glassblowing is an ancient industry and the earliest bottles were free-blown – another time-consuming technique that changed little over centuries. A mixture of sand, potash and lime would be heated in a crucible to the consistency of treacle, the blowpipe dipped and the adhering blob of glass mouth-blown to a hollow sphere. The semi-molten glass was then rolled on a stone or the blowpipe spun between the fingers to form a bottle shape. Once cool, the glass was sheared off from the blowpipe, the neck reheated and the lip rolled smooth. It was a lengthy and highly skilled process, which is why glass bottles remained expensive – meaning even the wealthy would send their own to be refilled by a wine merchant.

One clue that a bottle is hand-made is a circular scar at the base. These are known as 'pontil scars' and are part of the reason for the arched kick-up at the base of wine bottles: the 'island', with its last illusion of plenty. In order to form the neck, a hand-blown bottle would be held with a 'pontil rod' attached to the base, leaving a scar when the bottle was tapped free (glassblowers also knew the kick-up as a 'shove-up', from the way it was formed). It was the protruding pontil scar – along with the way bases sagged as they cooled – that meant a kick-up was the only way a free-blown bottle could stand flat.

As with the production of clay pipes, the first step in speeding up bottle making was the use of wooden moulds. The earliest were hollowed out from solid timber, but the design soon developed into two- and three-piece wooden moulds, and later hinged and more adaptable metal moulds. Each of these techniques left its mark on the glass and, of the bottles I'd found so far, most had a tell-tale seam down the side. On the oldest bottles this stopped short of the rim, and sometimes of the neck and shoulders too, showing that those parts were hand-applied to a mould-blown body. My favourite today was broken and a misted aqua: melted just a little in the kiln or a fire, its shoulder seams had shifted out of place, like a hastily pulled-on shirt.

The move to moulds brought a significant increase in the bottlemakers' output. As a result, the price of glass bottles began to fall, as manufacturers took their first steps towards mass production.

Another of the morning's favourites was a heavy glass bottle studded with barnacles inside and out. It had 'R WHITES' embossed on one side and on the other 'DEPOSIT CHARGED ON THIS BOTTLE'. Over the years I'd seen quite a few broken R. White's bottles here, often the heavy stoneware kind that once held ginger beer, which Robert White and his wife began selling in 1845 from a barrow in south London. Later they moved on to a market stall and over subsequent decades, like other drinks manufacturers, benefited from the falling price of sugar. By 1894, the company owned seven factories and, alongside the stoneware bottles of ginger beer, were also selling carbonated drinks in glass bottles.

From the start, the drinks' fizziness proved a problem for the glass manufacturers, as over time the accumulating pressure of the gas pushed out the corks or blew the bottoms off. This was the reason for the invention of a couple of the more curious and collectible bottle designs, including the torpedo-shaped 'Hamilton' bottles often seen lying on their sides in junk shops. Already, I'd found several of their rounded, almost indestructible ends part-buried in the mud, one embossed with the part-word SCHWEP. The insight behind the innovation was that, as torpedo bottles couldn't stand up, vendors would be forced to store them on their sides. By keeping the cork wet, this prevented shrinkage and maintained a good seal.

R. White's used an alternative design known as the Codd bottle, named for its inventor Hiram Codd. Another familiar sight in junk shops, Codd bottles have a marble trapped within the neck, which the pressure of the gas forces upwards to create a seal. To open and pour, the marble was pushed down, and the bottles could then be shaken to renew the seal. Sadly the few I'd lifted from the mud were broken at the neck and missing their marbles, which is common at dumps, as children would smash off the tops to get at them.

I'd collected more bottlenecks than usual, again for clues to their method of manufacture. On the more recent twentieth-century bottles the seam ran from the base right up through the lip, showing they were entirely made by machine. It was in 1903 that the first fully automated bottle machines began to appear and from then on glass bottles became increasingly uniform. As designs like the Codd could only be made by hand, manufacturers began phasing them out. Steadily those glass-blowers' flaws and defects began to disappear, along with a rich language of specific imperfection. Bottles no longer had stretch marks, crooked necks or wrinkles. They didn't bulge, wobble or sag, and were not marred – or to many a collector enhanced – by their tear-shaped blisters. Instead they came in standard, machine-made shapes.

Through the early 1900s the bottlemakers' output increased dramatically. As glass became cheaper to produce, manufacturers began using it to package more of their products. Tea, for example – previously weighed out at the shop and taken home in paper – could now be bought as a glass-bottled extract. Combined with rising incomes, the fall in prices meant shops began stocking readymade foods aimed at a much broader market. Among other things, the new machine-made glass bottles and jars now contained sauces and relishes, prepared baby foods, and meat- and fish pastes (ribbed Shippam's paste jars are particularly common finds at these turn-of-the-century dumps). Bottled meat extracts became especially popular, meaning women no longer had to spend hours in the kitchen boiling bones for stock.

By 1912, the machines could produce fifty bottles a minute. Along with improvements to Britain's road and rail networks – allowing nationwide distribution – this opened up the possibility of mass markets. Collectively these changes were sweeping, taking place throughout industry as manufacturers moved from using skilled craftsmen to specialist machines – deepening the shift away from muscle power to a reliance on fossils fuels. As output increased and prices came down, across the country more and more people could afford to buy a far wider range of products.

Before long, the supply of glass bottles was outstripping any possible demand for reuse. This shift to 'one-ways' also began affecting design, so that bottles and jars now appeared in increasingly odd and distinctive shapes, which were instantly recognizable but discouraged reuse (already today I'd passed over several broken brown globes that once held Bovril or Marmite). As a result, through the pre-war years, household bins contained an increasing amount of discarded glass – with a fair proportion from London ending up on the Estuary marshes.

By noon I was hot and slightly dazed. With no shade from the midsummer sun, the marshes had that blasted feel I remembered from childhood. It was soon so hot that even the lower shore had begun to dry out, at least at the surface. The bladderwrack had hardened to salt-crusted greys and its monochrome worlds glittered like winter. When I moved one stiff curtain to check the embossing on a bottle – TONIC – a shore crab darted out and scuttled off sideways. Elsewhere a sea snail filled the mouth of a sheared-off bottleneck like a cork, and another group clustered together beneath the rim of a mud-filled cream pot. Everywhere, creatures waited out the exposure of low tide in damp lairs beneath broken crockery, seeking shelter from the sun and poking gulls. When I lifted part of a teapot, tiny worms and shrimps were left wriggling in a spout-shaped pool.

There was another strangeness out here too: glass that had burned or melted in weird and wonderful shapes. (Some of it was hardcore used as insulation on the brick kilns, although this so-called 'bonfire-glass' can also come from post-incineration waste or burning-off at tips.) More than once I saw the features of distorted faces in a bottle lying in the mud: the sagging mouth of a kick-up, with barnacle teeth; a big hooked nose protruding from a pool. Other bottles had bubbled or turned opaque in the heat; some had wrinkled like elephant skin, or taken on the shapes of surrounding hardcore. In the midday sun, much of it was also clothed in the Halloween textures of dried seaweed: felted mats and torn shrouds, sun-stiffened bladderwrack drapes.

In this sheltered creek there was so much junk it was almost a reef, albeit a reef of shifting crocks. In these gentle backwater currents, though, when objects move it is rarely far; I'd found some heavy bottles with their top sides encrusted with big old barnacles, suggesting they'd barely moved at all. I headed further up the beach then, picking my way across this odd shore where so much was hidden; where, as is so common in estuaries, our waste had become part of the landscape itself.

Later that afternoon, for the very first time, I got my 'eye in' for inkwells. Altogether I found three, each one melted and distorted. The first I found entirely by chance: a sagging 'boat ink' lying at the surface, with twin grooves along its shoulders to rest a refillable pen. After that I recognized their shape more easily, even when little was visible. The second was similar, with the rough, burst-off lip of a disposable 'penny ink'. This kind of lip was easy for the glassblowers to make: when finished, they simply allowed a bubble to form at the end of the blow-pipe and snapped off the bottle as it burst; the rough-edged lip was then plugged with a cork and sealing wax. The third was much higher on the beach. It lay beside a blackened ridge of what looked like kiln remains – a fire-welded mass of burnt bricks fused with broken pottery and glass. Quite different to the rest, this last one had turned opaque in intense heat, yet retained much of its original octagonal shape.

Inkwells are common finds at Victorian and pre-war dumps, and reflect rising levels of literacy. In 1880 education had been made compulsory in England for children between the ages of five and ten. In 1893 the school leaving age was raised to eleven and by the turn of the century it was twelve – meaning an increasing proportion of adults were able to read.

This was another crucial step in the consumer revolution. Together with technical advances in printing and reproduction, it meant advertising could now reach a far broader range of potential customers, making it easier to market those mass-produced goods. This brought a surge in printed adverts, which filled increasing amounts of space in newspapers, magazines and even novels. For the growing middle classes, with more time and money on their hands, shopping was an increasingly popular leisure activity, and with the rise in literacy more people now recognized brands.

Once a product's name and claims could be printed onto packaging – paper, glass, tin, ceramic – it also became possible to influence customers at the point of sale. This transformed the purpose of packaging. Whereas before it had been mainly a means of transporting, storing and protecting goods, now it was also a way to sell them.

Some of the most popular finds from Victorian dumps are transfer-printed pot lids, and although Bottle Beach has been picked clean of these collectible treasures over decades, back in the 1970s and 1980s they were common here. In time, the expanding range of Victorian readymade products included shaving creams, toothpastes, lip salves and cold creams. Dandruff pomades stood alongside Imperial Hair Dye and 'delicately scented' hair restorers 'Made from Genuine Russian Bear's Grease'. Some of the more collectible lids and jars advertise 'never-failing ointment', 'miraculous salve' and an 'infallible cure for all diseases'.

These quack medicines and 'cure-alls' were among the earliest products to be widely advertised. They were available over the counter and manufacturers were not required to list ingredients, which were often harmful. The active ingredients in Mrs Winslow's Soothing Syrup, for instance – branded 'The Mother's

Friend' and recommended for teething infants – were alcohol and morphine. (Its unsurprising effectiveness proved so popular with parents that, despite acquiring the nickname 'baby killer', it continued to sell widely in Britain right through to the 1930s.) Perhaps best known in Victorian times, though, were Holloway's Pills and Ointment. Thomas Holloway's success was down to his pioneering belief in relentless advertising and promotion, which brought huge increases in sales. With little or no regulation of the rapidly growing advertising industry, companies were free to make their unsubstantiated claims as wild as they liked. Consisting largely of beeswax and lanolin, Holloway's Ointment was promoted as a cure (more or less alphabetically) for 'Bad Legs, Bad Breasts, Burns, Bunions, Bite of Mosquito and Sand-Flies, Scalds, Chiego-foot, Chilblains, Cancers, Elephantiasis, Fistulas, Gout, Glandular Swellings, Lumbago, Piles, Rheumatism, Sore-throats, Sore-heads, Scurvy, Tumours, Ulcers, Yaws, Sore Nipples'.

The phenomenal success of some of these early brands inspired an explosion of new products. Most were aimed at women, with advertisers particularly keen to tap into the middle class's new obsession with cleanliness. Through the work of investigative journalists and campaigners such as Edwin Chadwick and George 'Graveyard' Walker, the spread of disease was primarily seen as a result of the filthy state of slum housing, sewers and graveyards. In the wake of the resultant sanitary movement, cleanliness had become firmly linked in the public mind with morality and respectability, which was gold to the advertisers. Images of the idealized housewife and mother – and her radiant babies – could now be used to sell everything from soap and disinfectant to polish and clothes whitener.

Before the nineteenth century, even the wealthy didn't regularly wash their bodies, often illustrated by the observation that Queen Elizabeth I was unusual for taking a bath regularly every month 'whether she needs it or not'. The poor often did little more than wash their hands and face (amongst the poorest, some were unable to change their clothes as they owned only one set at a time). By the 1890s, though, British habits had changed, and we were buying an estimated 260,000 tonnes of soap a year. It was no longer cut from a bar at the shop counter and wrapped in plain paper; now, like so much else, it came in branded packaging.

Pear's Soap in particular was continually promoted. In one series of images from the 1880s, a white boy stands over a black boy sitting in a bathtub. He holds out a bar of Pear's Soap, as if teaching the black boy to wash. In the accompanying 'after' image, a magical cleansing has taken place – the white boy holds up a mirror so the other can see that, now he's washed, only his head remains black. With Pear's Soap, the colour has been washed from his skin like dirt, revealing a pure, white body underneath. For the Victorians, soap had become deeply symbolic: of progress and moral salvation, of the civilizing mission of empire. Cleanliness was definitely next to Godliness. It was a virtue, a defining difference between the civilized and the uncivilized – which applied as much to the poor as it did to 'natives' from the colonies. By that time, my great-great-grandfather Tom Tolladay – orphaned at thirteen in the slums – was a coalman. And like the Victorian dustmen and the chimney sweeps (who appear in another Pear's advert), coalmen were a perfect representation of 'the great unwashed'.

All the while, Britain's middle classes continued to expand, as rising prosperity from trade and manufacturing created white-collar jobs such as clerks and managers. As in the Georgian era, this increase in upward mobility brought a renewed emphasis on being seen to do and buy the right things. The newly rich in particular were often keen to avoid errors in both manners and taste, and as more people began to follow fashion, the social ideal became increasingly focussed on material possessions. Ideally a man could now support his family on a single wage, and it was a mark of social standing if his wife didn't need to go out to work. So a major way for women to demonstrate status became through the home. By the turn of the century, middle-class parlours were crowded with fashionable new purchases, many resembling family heirlooms: oil paintings, pianos and grandfather clocks, stuffed animals and overstuffed chairs. Dark sideboards displayed their cut glass, ornaments and trinkets – and elaborately decorated china like that now in pieces at my feet.

I was wandering through the shallows, the sun glinting off submerged crockery, when I heard voices behind me. I looked around to see three women and a young girl walking along the flood bank at the top of the shore. The girl began to hang back.

'Can I go down on the beach?' she asked.

She was about five and stopped to stare down at me.

'No,' one of the women said.

The girl pointed to a small patch of beach that was more shingle than pottery. 'Just that bit down there?'

The women stopped. They glanced over at me and lowered their voices, so I couldn't make out what was said.

'No,' the woman said more loudly, going back to pull the girl by the hand. 'You get dirty doing nothing.'

By then the tide was on its way in, creeping ashore over sun-warmed mud. In the distance, the moored yachts had begun to right themselves. Reaching down for a piece of plate-rim decorated with ivy leaves, I was surprised at the water's warmth. Around me other fragments lay on the creek bed, printed with roses and strawberry leaves, their broken edges furred a brilliant algal green. I trod on, with ribbons of gutweed unfurling from botanical designs to drift lazily at my ankles, through surreal underwater gardens.

An hour later I was done, and headed up the shore to look through what I'd found. At the top, shards of pottery were now set fast into the cracked, baked mud, its surface dusted with salt crystals that patterned it like lace. I sat down and set the pottery fragments out on the ground one by one. Blue flowers and grape vines. The scalloped edge of a saucer; a beautifully detailed oak leaf. A teacup handle almost too small for a finger. The words 'Marmalade', 'International Club', 'Lambeth'. Then some hand-painted fruit on a Spode plate. Beneath the crazed surface of the glaze, some of the fragments had yellowed with age; others were scarred with red burn marks. Many of the images were strikingly intricate, and once again it was industry's technological advances that brought such designs within reach of the many. Like glass blowing, painting pottery by hand was a time-consuming skill that kept prices high. With the move to transfer-printing, the use of engraved plates meant an image could be repeatedly pressed against ceramic surfaces. Once again the increased output brought prices down, and it was no longer just the wealthy who could own elaborately decorated china.

Finally, I laid out several fragments of blue-and-white oriental landscapes. This style became common in the nineteenth century: a cheaper imitation of Chinese porcelain, which had finally been copied in the previous century. The last piece showed a pair of birds. This is a central motif of Willow Pattern, that most popular of oriental styles. Specific elements of these familiar waterside landscapes also include three or four figures on a bridge, a tree bearing fruit, a pagoda and a crooked fence. The story behind the design was first published in England in 1849 and was said to have come from an ancient Chinese fable. According to this, a mandarin's daughter falls in love with a commoner against her father's wishes. So the mandarin banishes the lover and plans his daughter's marriage to a duke. The lovers elope and live happily on a secluded island for many years, until they're found by the duke and killed. The gods, though, are moved by the strength of the couple's love and transform them into doves. Each element of a Willow Pattern design was said to represent a part of this ancient oriental myth – except that it didn't. The legend turned out to have been invented, decades after the design first appeared, as a sales promotion by English porcelain manufacturers, which worked with spectacular success (the design is still produced in bulk today).

With rising competition and so much potential for expansion, a nascent marketing industry was just beginning to discover how many ways we could be persuaded to buy.

5

Swale Marshes

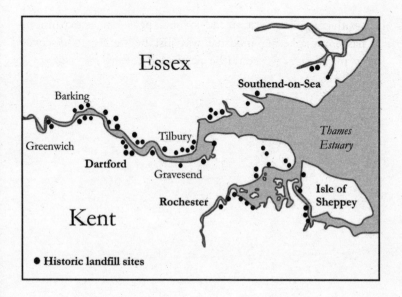

Driving back along the marsh road the following evening, I slowed down for a better look at a barge wreck. Like others, this would originally have been hulked at the muddy creek edge, perhaps after the brickworks closed, but in the stillness of this quiet backwater the saltmarsh was encroaching seawards. So, unlike the blackened hulls out on the mudflats, this one appeared to have beached on dry land. Silvered by the weather, the last of its exposed timbers were gradually sinking into pillows of cordgrass, settling down to become part of the marsh's creeping advance.

I was glancing back for one last look when I saw the couch. Down on the saltmarsh below the road, it was blue and facing out towards the estuary. In Cornwall I occasionally come across incongruous chairs in the middle of nowhere – often facing out to sea – so my first thought was that it had been put there for someone to sit and look out at the view. I grinned and pulled over. In late sunlight, the verge was a wall of cricket song. Feeling tired from sleeping on the driveway, I poured the last of the flask's tepid coffee and headed out to the couch. It was only as I sat down that I saw the matching chair face-down further out – and realized they'd been fly-tipped.

There was even a stereo rusting in the mud. I shifted position so it was just out of sight. The rubbish wasn't a surprise, though, as from the layby the previous day I'd glimpsed a heap of wet carpet and several bald tyres. Unlike the litter in the layby verges, these were things people had driven out here specially to dump. As it has for centuries, the relative remoteness of the estuary marshes still suggests an obvious 'away'.

Taking a similar route to the Bovril Boats and rough stuff before it, London's twentieth-century rubbish also flowed east along the Thames into Kent and Essex: downriver and downwind. While landfill remained a cheap and easy solution to the problem of burgeoning waste, London boroughs continued buying up marshland along the estuary to bury it. At the time there were few concerns around siting the dumps near water, on Britain's coasts and low-lying estuaries. In the Thames Estuary alone there are thought to be more than fifty disused sites at risk of flooding and erosion, with a number that have already breached. Over the water at Tilbury, vast swathes of London's historic waste can already be seen hanging from wave-scoured riverbanks and scattered on shore.

Earlier in the year I'd taken my mum to visit an eroding site with me. As I'm happy to spend hours searching, I'm often wary of taking anyone along, but from previous trips I knew that some of the finds were likely to date from her 1940s and 1950s childhood. The forecast that day was bleak, with an emphasis on wind-chill, but as we stood in the car park piling on extra layers and waterproofs, I was hoping for finds that might spark memories of those post-war years. As the 1950s in particular saw another big shift in British attitudes towards consumption and waste, I also hoped to find traces of those changes on the shore, with the eroding landfill exposing its once-buried record of an era.

The dump's contents had been washing out onto the shore for over a decade. Our first glimpse was from the steps leading down to the concrete sea wall and there, sheltered as we were from the wind, when the sun came out it was almost warm. I glanced over at my mum and she pulled a face: at our bulky, overdressed gait; at the sound of rubbing waterproofs over too many layers.

As beachcombing is often best during inclement weather, more than once I'd trudged down those steps in the rain. A few months earlier it had been with my eleven-year-old daughter, when the two of us spent a couple of hours grubbing about on the shore with freezing hands, our jeans stiff in the wet, her red hair plastered to the outside of her hood (but all was well as she found blue poison glass and a fool's-gold fossil).

On reaching the beach below the dump with my mum, it was clear that the cliff falls were fresh. The clay was sodden and slick, with a glistening layer still covering the stones at the top of the shore. Its undulating surface had been sculpted by recent high tides and was studded with broken pottery and glass. It was here, on a previous visit, that I'd eased an emerald green poison bottle free of the mud. Rinsed clean, it proved to be machine-made and ridged to warn of dangerous contents; most appealing of all was its gentle sag, presumably caused by burning-off at the tip.

In the years since the landfill breached, locals have found all sorts washed from the toe of this cliff, from cookers, a glass eye and a golliwog moneybox to rusting boilers, asbestos tiles and the 'full evolutionary sequence' of Marmite jars.

I'd not been searching long when I picked up a vulcanite bottle stopper. These are common finds and I already had quite a few from the Thames. Yet there is always something appealing about them – in the feel of the material, in the way they've worn, in the variety of logos for old breweries and beers. Invented in 1872, they were made from heat-treated ('vulcanized') rubber and used widely on beer bottles before the rise of the familiar, single-use 'crown cap'. A favourite in my collection at home has the words 'WAR GRADE' imprinted around its scooped-out centre: a modification that meant less material was needed to make them.

Another kind that is particularly collectible was produced by the St Austell Brewery, which until the 1930s sold a bottled ale with its vulcanite stopper imprinted with a swastika. Until the rise of the Nazi party, this was commonly used in both Britain and Europe as a symbol of good fortune. It is an ancient design, featuring on everything from a 12,000-year-old ivory figurine to artefacts created by the Ancient Greeks, Vikings, medieval Christians, Buddhists and Hindus. Prior to its appropriation by Nazism, the swastika also featured on Coca-Cola and Boy Scout memorabilia. But by the outbreak of the Second World War, it had become an emblem of fascism, its meaning changed for good in the West. Unsurprisingly, the St Austell Brewery felt compelled to grind out the swastikas from all existing stocks of its vulcanite stoppers – so they resembled those that were 'war grade' to conserve resources.

In the decades leading up to the First World War, recycling had been in steep decline. From the late nineteenth century, the combination of cheap raw materials and machine-made, mass-produced goods changed public attitudes to waste. Moving away from older practices of conservation, recycling and reuse, a new generation was learning to throw away and replace.

Yet with the war years came a golden era of salvage. The Second World War in particular brought national salvage drives, new laws on waste and patriotic propaganda campaigns such as 'Make Do and Mend'. Recycling was made compulsory: for rags, paper, glass, string, metal, bones and food waste. Scrap-metal drives not only removed the iron railings from parks and gardens, but also required the public to search cupboards and attics for unused pots and pans. These would be melted down, they were told, and used to build tanks and weapons. Old kettles and coat hangers could be 'turned into Spitfires'. 'One envelope makes fifty cartridge wads,' proclaimed campaign leaflets, and 'a single chop bone provides cordite for two cartridges'. Communal waste bins appeared on street corners to take food scraps for pigs (new 'pig clubs' were springing up everywhere, from bomb sites and school fields to the Hyde Park Police piggery and a London destructor yard). The public response to these national salvage drives was so enthusiastic that wartime recycling reached levels of 'near frenzy'.

My mum was a toddler at the end of the war, so she grew up in the post-war years of shortages and continued rationing to pay off Britain's war debts. Yet without government salvage drives to combat complacency, levels of recycling began to fall dramatically. After six years of war, the public's enthusiasm had waned and a number of campaigns designed to reinvigorate the wartime spirit proved ineffective.

For London's dustmen, though, this was a welcome opportunity to start 'tooting' again, a practice said to have an ancestry as old as the first dustheap. My grandad became a dustman after the Second World War. His brother-in-law – Uncle Dick – got him in, as he'd been a dustman for years and by then had the treasured job of house clearances, which at the time were still done with a horse and cart. As well as his local Walworth streets, my grandad's rounds took him up through the Elephant and Castle and across Bermondsey to Borough Market by the Thames.

To the dustmen, anything salvaged from the rubbish was 'toot' (pronounced as in foot). I spent some time trying to decide how to spell this, as although everyone in the family knows the word, I couldn't find anyone who'd ever seen it written down. Later, I found others had spelt it 'tut' – as in put – and sometimes 'tot'. It seems its origins lie in the use of 'tot' as a slang term for bone, with the nineteenth-century bone-pickers known as 'tot hunters' and the rag-and-bone men as 'totters'.

Between the wars, the dustmen's horses and carts were gradually replaced by motorized dustcarts. By my grandad's time any toot fished out of the rubbish was thrown up on top of the truck. In the neighbouring borough of Lambeth this was more official, with the council renting trailers to its dustmen for their toot, which were towed along behind the dustcarts. Like the old dustyard system, any salvage was then sorted back at the yard after hours, with contractors calling in to pay the dustmen directly. As with the sorters at the old dustyards, many of the dustmen had a speciality, and my grandad's was pewter – often plates and mugs considered old-fashioned by then – which he took to the local toot shop.

I was fortunate, that day on the shore with my mum. Recent storms had stripped the beach of much of its sand and shingle, revealing far more from the dump than usual. Over an hour or so, in intermittent rain, I picked up forks and spark plugs, chair castors and a brass tap, a fish knife and a flat iron. Amongst the finer shingle I also found zip pulls, old fly buttons and a 1955 shilling, as well as a tiny brass propeller and the front leg of a lead toy horse.

There were also a couple of metal tube-mouths – one lead and the other aluminium. These are common finds at dumps of this age, likely to be from toothpaste tubes, and spanning several stages in their evolution. As manufacturers moved away from the Victorian era's jars of toothpowders (often containing abrasives such as salt, soot or brick dust), the first toothpaste tubes were inspired by artists' paint tubes and were made from lead. With the introduction of wartime restrictions, though, manufacturers speeded up the switch to aluminium.

Entirely engrossed, I was rummaging happily through the finds bag when I looked up suddenly to scan the shore – realizing I'd lost all track of time as well as my mum. It took a while to spot her. There were several figures on the beach by then and, like the rest, she was zipped to the chin in waterproofs. But there she was: crouched mid-shore with her head down, completely absorbed in whatever she was doing. I felt a rush of gratitude. Struggling over to her with my bag of finds – as well as three rusted irons now – I found she'd collected nails and laid them out on a rock. When I showed her my own finds, she recognized many of the domestic things from her childhood: a hand-turned meat mincer; part of a treadle sewing machine; the flat iron heated on a range; the heavy, rusted remains of two early electric irons. Back home, these would join previous finds from this beach, my favourite a beautifully sea-worn mangle roller.

Together, these objects were a reminder of just how different my nan's life was to both my mum's and my own. In comparison, she worked incredibly hard at home, spending most of the week scrubbing and wringing clothes, mending and ironing, cooking and shopping for food. To get the best price on a piece of meat she would trawl every butcher's shop and stall at East Lane Market, and use every last scrap. She stewed pig's trotters and made dripping, boiled bones and scooped out the marrow with the end of a spoon. For my grandad – with his extra money from tips and selling toot – it was a mark of pride that he was able to hand his weekly wage packet over to my nan.

In those post-war years, poorer families in particular also spent quite a bit of their time on repairs. Shoes were resoled many times – my grandad used discarded factory machine belts – and old clothes were altered to fit others in the family. Frayed collars would be 'turned' and re-stitched. Rags were saved and every button on a worn-out garment cut off to be used again (as children, both my mum and I spent many happy hours sorting through my nan's button box). Bed sheets were 'side-to-middled' – re-stitched so the thinning centre was moved to the edge – and the same would be done with carpets. Anything bought was built to last and if something broke it could often be repaired by someone local. Glass bottles were returned to the shop for a deposit and children's toys often made at home. When I showed my mum the lead horse's leg, she recalled the lead toy animals her dad had made for her and her siblings, and then struggled to remember any toys they had that were not homemade.

As was common at the time, even the bathwater was repeatedly reused. For mum's family, bath night was Fridays, when the tin bath would be moved into the scullery and topped-up with hot water between bathers. The order was strict and based on a general perception of cleanliness: my nan in first, eldest daughter second, mum third, boys next and – due to his job – my grandad last.

The clothes he wore for work had often been found on his rounds – tied with string if they didn't fit – and smelt so bad that, rather than being put in the wash with everything else, they were often thrown away. I presume that working in found clothes was common practice for dustmen at the time, and I'd read of the Famous Bin Men of Lyme: for a time in the 1950s, the town's dustmen became tabloid phenomenon, as they worked their rounds wearing discarded bowler hats and frock coats.

As my grandad's rounds included his own street – my mum remembers hanging onto the back of the dustcart to get to primary school – he'd drop off his toot when he passed the house. I got a better idea of this on a recent visit to my mum's brother Eddy. He still lives in south London and almost as soon as we arrived, the two of them were reminiscing about the things my grandad would leave at the house.

'You'd hear the door go and Mum's face would drop,' Eddy said. 'Then she'd shoot out into the passage to see what he'd left.'

These weren't always things he'd sell at the toot shop, just anything of value left out for the dustmen – or, as Eddy put it, through my grandad 'coming to some arrangement'.

My mum recalled paving slabs, and another time, 'Bags and

bags of defrosted peas. Back then, shop fridges were always breaking down.'

Eddy remembered iced coconut.

'It was pink, great slabs of it. I remember that tasting strange.' He shook his head. 'Though I think we were immune by then.'

Both of them remembered the three-piece suite they had in the front room.

'He got that on his rounds,' Eddy said. 'Green tweed. We had it for years. Not the sort of thing we'd normally have. And old tools, things like that – anything saleable. He'd never tell you where it came from, just said he'd "acquired" it. He always said that. Things "just happened to be lying about".'

I caught both of them making the same face.

'Not sure how close they were to the bin sometimes,' Eddy said. 'And what about that gold ring? The one he gave Mum when they were sixteen. There's no way he bought that.'

I'd heard of this ring before. My mum had showed it to me a few weeks earlier, turning it so the tiny sliver of diamond caught the light, as she talked about her parents' childhoods. They'd grown up around the corner from each other near East Lane Market, my nan in Revesby Street and my grandad in Beddome Street: the one described by Charles Booth's researcher as 'poor, doors open, general labourers'.

Beddome Street was where my grandad was born, and the few things my mum knows of his childhood came from my nan. As well as talking of his scavenger dad, she said his mum couldn't read or write, and 'birthed and laid out the dead'. She said my grandad often went hungry as a child and stole bread to feed himself and his mum. At that point, my mum recalled, my nan would always say, 'But he wasn't a thief.'

During our visit to Eddy, when anyone spoke of my grandad there was warmth in their expression – which, as usual, slipped away at the mention of his dad. As the eldest son, he was also named Tom Tolladay.

'He was big and had very blue eyes,' Eddy told me. 'Never knew his own strength, people said. And he was always shouting.'

I was told once that 'he earnt nothing and drank it', but I know little more than that. Whenever I've asked, people have often seemed uncomfortable talking about him, and several times – as the subject was changed – I got the impression he was a violent drunk.

Beyond those fragments, all I know is my mum's description of being taken to his flat as a young child, when her dad went over to shave him. Mum's older sister, Sylvie, still lives around the corner from Eddy, so that same day we'd also called in to see her.

'Dad's sister used to make him go,' Sylvie said. 'And he always took one of us children with him. I always thought he was scared to go on his own.'

By the time my mum was old enough to be taken along, Tom was widowed and approaching eighty. He lived at nearby Blendon Row, a slum tenement that became infamous before it was pulled down, where dustmen clearing the rubbish chutes would tie string around their trouser legs to stop the rats running up them. On hearing this, I wondered whether that post-war generation of dustmen were still calling those neighbourhoods 'dead pieces'.

My mum remembered her visits vividly.

'Scared the living daylights out of me,' she said. Part of the reason for this was that it was always pitch-dark in the stairwells.

'People took the light bulbs. You had to feel your way up the stairs.'

From the flat, my grandad had to go two floors down to get water for the shave, and would leave my mum with her grandad. Although there are twelve years between Sylvie and my mum – and I got the impression they'd not talked of this before – their memories were almost identical. Both described sitting with their faces up close to the window glass, staring out at the 'swing park' playground below, afraid of the rasp of his breathing behind them (he too had a progressive lung disease, exacerbated by the London smogs, which had killed both his father and grandfather by the age of fifty).

I learned later that the Blendon Row estate and its rats featured in the classic 1972 documentary *We Was All One*, which looked at the effects of the slum clearances sweeping London at the time. The copy I found was grainy, shot in muted Seventies colour, and I watched the scenes of Blendon Row over and over again. Although the film was made two decades after my mum was taken there, I was struck by how similar the place was to the one she described. The grim tenement block is used to illustrate the squalor of the slums before they're pulled down, and early scenes linger on its smog-blackened exterior and boarded-up ground floor, on rats that flash along shadowy corridors.

The nearby terraced streets where my nan and grandad grew up were also pulled down in the clearances. When we talked of them at Eddy's, he disappeared for a while and came back with an ancient London *A–Z*, slipping it carefully from a brittle plastic sleeve. As he turned the yellowed pages to find Walworth, several came loose. On the cramped streets around East Lane Market, the print was so small that none of us could read it. Eventually – with all three of us peering through the same big magnifying glass – we found the two streets. My grandad's was a cul-de-sac, a turning off my nan's street, and both Eddy and my mum remembered it.

'Mum didn't like going down there.'

'No. Because they all sat outside on chairs.'

Which is when I remembered the phrase 'doors open' in the notebook of Booth's researcher, implying there were too many people living in each house for them all to be inside at once.

On the Booth Poverty Maps, those streets around the market

are labelled simply 'Poor'. Yet for those living there, it was of course more nuanced than that. My nan's street might be Poor, but it wasn't as poor as my grandad's. Her dad worked as a print setter and as the print unions were strong he could support his twelve children more or less on a single wage (his wife, from a family of shoemakers, also did piecework, sewing the leather uppers onto factory workers' clogs). Growing up around the corner from my grandad, my nan had known him since childhood, long before he gave her the gold ring. Both my mum and Eddy remembered my nan saying how angry her mum was when she saw the ring, and that my nan was told to give it back. She obviously didn't, and three years later they were married, from which time – by all accounts – my nan kept a very white, respectable front step.

Since childhood, I've always loved visiting my aunt Sylvie's house, because it smells of books. On that last visit, she'd said the only reason she went to grammar school was because of some kind of dustman's favour my grandad had done for a local greengrocer. At the time – as the eldest daughter – she was expected to leave school as soon as possible to help out at home. Yet following this favour for the greengrocer, my nan and grandad were invited to his house for a meal, and in conversation his wife said proudly that her daughter would be going to grammar school. Which changed my nan's mind. So Sylvie was allowed to take her eleven-plus exam and went on to the same Bermondsey grammar school as my mum twelve years later – situated between the soap factory, the glue works and the tannery.

On leaving school, Sylvie worked at Bermondsey Library, where she met her future husband, Peter. A fellow librarian, softly spoken with a gentle manner, he had grown up on a better-off street. My mum remembers the first few times Sylvie brought him home for tea, and how my nan was keen for the family not to do the wrong thing. Before they arrived at the house, she would take Mum and her brothers aside and remind them that, once they sat down to the meal, they must all wait to see what Peter did first – and then do the same thing.

I love this. And I like how it sits alongside another memory my mum has, this time of her dad's side of the family: of bumping into his sister in the street soon after I was born. This was Uncle Dick's wife – 'always wore dead animals round her neck' – who looked down at me lying in my pram and said loudly, 'Aw. Bloody lovely little fucker, that.'

As I write this now, the lead horse's leg is beside me on the desk. It reminds me of my mum as a child, playing with her handed-down lead animals in those post-war years. With my own daughter leaving primary school this year, I think with unease of the number of toys that have passed through our house this past decade and a half – and how many were made of plastic.

Although hard to imagine now, the first plastics were conceived as a means of protecting the natural world, by reducing the pressure on scarce natural resources. The invention of the very first plastic – celluloid – came in response to concerns that the dwindling number of elephants (due to European and American demand for their tusks) was affecting the supply of ivory. A growing Victorian middle class had brought rising demand for this versatile material, which was used to make everything from combs and piano keys to the handles of umbrellas. One of its main uses was for billiard balls, and in 1863 a newspaper advertisement placed by a billiards supplier offered a 'handsome fortune' to anyone able to invent a replacement for ivory.

Several years later, after numerous experiments in a workshop behind his house, the amateur American inventor James Wesley Hyatt finally created the first plant-based synthetic plastic, celluloid. Unfortunately, it didn't work well for billiard balls, in part because the noise they made when clacking together was too much like a gunshot. But as the first practical and commercial plastic, celluloid did make his fortune. Much of the material's early appeal lay in its ability to mimic limited and expensive natural materials: creamy ivory, veined marble, mottled tortoiseshell. As one of Hyatt's company pamphlets claimed, 'It will no longer be necessary to ransack the earth in pursuit of substances which are constantly growing scarcer.'

Bakelite, invented by Leo Baekeland in America in 1907, was the first fully synthetic plastic. Again, it was conceived as a replacement for a natural substance – this time shellac, a resin secreted by an Asian beetle and used as an electrical insulator. However, shellac's time-consuming production made it expensive and, again, it was difficult for the natural world to satisfy growing demand. Baekeland's hard brown Bakelite – made, like modern plastics, from a by-product of fossil fuels – did the job just as well. Promoted by its inventor as 'the material of a thousand uses', in time it became ubiquitous in British homes – in plugs and light fittings, and other durable products such as radios, ashtrays and telephones.

After Bakelite came other more versatile plastics. In a flood of discoveries leading up to the Second World War, the new polymer chemists found they could turn fossil-fuel by-products into everything from polystyrene, nylon and PVC to the now-ubiquitous polyethylene. Manufacturers loved these new materials. Both malleable and durable, they were also versatile, cheap and easy to produce. It was during the war that they first came into their own, with nylon replacing silk in parachutes, and plastics becoming essential components in everything from helmets and bazookas to radar and the atomic bomb. With the war's end, though, this boom began to dry up, leaving the plastics manufacturers seeking new markets.

As well as the material innovations, there were now also

faster methods of production – in particular injection moulding, where the raw plastic pellets could be melted and shaped in a single action. As an illustration of rising productivity, a now-famous photograph appeared in *The Times*, showing father and son combmakers standing beside their respective daily output of combs. Beside the father is a neat stack of 350 celluloid combs, whereas the son is surrounded by the 10,000 plastic combs a machine could produce in a day. Crucially, such large quantities meant plastic goods were now cheap to produce.

My mum has a clear memory of seeing her first plastic comb. When she was a teenager in the 1950s, her eldest brother Alby worked for Shell on plastics research. One evening he came home from work with the comb, and she remembers the whole family marvelling at how far it would bend without breaking. At least to begin with, plastic was also seen as modern and cool. For the manufacturers, it was in ordinary homes that future opportunity lay. And now – with strong links to the powerful oil industry – they'd become bigger players. All they needed to do was persuade us to buy.

For a generation who had lived through the war, it didn't come naturally to discard things or buy more than was necessary (my grandparents, used to repairing everything and side-to-middling their carpets, would not be an easy sell). So people had to be taught to consume. One answer lay in more sophisticated advertising. Again this focussed mainly on women, with adverts now common in lifestyle magazines, at the movies and on commercial television. By the 1950s adverts were showing how the new wonder plastics – from Tupperware to wipe-clean Formica – could revolutionize lives. New standards of hygiene were promised, along with freedom from the drudgery of time-consuming household tasks.

This was accompanied by a flood of electrical innovations: fridges and freezers removing the need to shop every day; ovens, irons, washing machines and food mixers; even – for a few –

the first dishwashers. It was another energy revolution, a major shift in the way we used the ancient sunlight stored in fossil fuels. Electricity, generated by coal-fired power stations, was now connected to homes, providing ordinary people with the muscle-power of dozens of slaves.

If the promise of convenience and saved time was not enough, there was also the seduction of modern styles. The new gadgets came in chrome and cool enamel colours, with sleek lines and organic, space-age shapes. The drab 1940s kitchen was now a thing of the past. A decade on, people had tired of post-war austerity and wages were rising; it was time to let the good times roll.

As standards of living continued to rise, the new mood saw a bright future for all. Comfort and convenience were no longer the preserves of the wealthy, with products once considered luxuries now seen as basic requirements. The cost of production was falling fast, due not only to increased automation and technological advance, but also cheap oil and the new economies of scale. Goods rolled from assembly lines, exploding onto consumer markets like never before. It seemed the optimism of those early inventors had not been misplaced: the new synthetic materials – products of our human ingenuity – had unleashed unlimited potential for growth. In 1957, Prime Minister Harold Macmillan captured the mood of the nation:

> Let us be frank about it: most of our people have never had it so good. Go round the country, go to the industrial towns, go to the farms, and you will see a state of prosperity such as we have never had in my lifetime – nor indeed in the history of this country.

Swept up in a worldwide economic boom, Britain had entered what is often known as the Golden Age of Capitalism. In so many ways the 1950s can be seen as a turning point, sometimes described as the Great Acceleration. From around the time my mum's family were bending their first plastic comb, a wide variety of graphs charting human activity show sharp, sustained growth: data collated recently by the International Geosphere–Biosphere Programme show that this growth included everything from consumption, carbon emissions and world population to pollution and the use of plastics and natural resources.

To make space for all these new modern purchases, we also had to grow more comfortable with the idea of throwing away. In tandem with the increase in production, the modernization of refuse collection also gathered pace. Where metal bins were once shouldered into open dustcarts, the trucks were now covered to reduce the nuisance of smells and spills. The 1950s also saw the introduction of black plastic sacks and rear-loading dustcarts, with their various mechanisms to chew and compact the rubbish. Increasingly, our refuse was whisked efficiently away from the kerbside – whether by my grandad in south London or the bowler-hatted binmen of Lyme.

All the while, the language of the industry was changing too. In time, incineration and sorting became 'resource recovery', landfill could be 'sanitary' and the whole process was referred to as the 'waste stream' – redolent of those shining rivers and waterways that from the very beginning had spirited away our waste.

By the time we'd been on the beach for a couple of hours, my mum's lips were beginning to turn mauve with cold, so I began packing up (noticing that she was leaving her nails behind). On the way back to the car, I fished around in my coat pocket for several bits I'd kept back to show her: a fork with the tines snapped off; the jagged remains of a knife; a coin with a chunk bitten out. In each case the damage looked violent, not the result of decades in the ground or on a beach. I'd found similarly broken metal there before and wondered how it might have happened.

'Chewed up by a dustcart?' I asked now – something I hadn't considered before.

'Could be,' my mum said. Neither of us could think of anything else likely to have torn the metal apart with so much force.

We paused at the top to look back at the shore, my mum saying how much her dad's job had changed by the time she left school, and how he hated the modernizations.

'Though he did like one,' she said. 'They gave all the dustmen uniforms: trousers, and donkey jackets with leather patches on the back. He loved that – went straight out and sold it.'

Of all the changes, she said he most disliked the new compactor trucks, for the way they affected the scavenging.

She shook her head, handing me back the mangled fork.

'Dad couldn't see any point in dusting after that.'

In the months since, I've kept my finds from that day together in a box, and realize, now, that they've acquired a curious value. Although most are broken or corroded – and not remotely saleable – they prompted memories and wayward conversations. They allowed a way in, a precious glimpse of things I may otherwise never have known. My mum is seventy-five now and there won't always be the chance to ask.

From the blue fly-tipped couch I looked out across the marsh. Around me, other dumped junk lay half-hidden in the cordgrass: more frayed carpet, plastic sheeting, a work boot – things I'd only gradually come to notice as I sat there; things that hadn't even made it to landfill. The more I looked the more I saw, and in the soft, late light it felt grimly insidious. Just how much of our rubbish was out there – from fly-tipped junk to the marsh's unnatural waste-filled hills?

On a map marking the south-east's historic landfill sites in red, the dots cluster like a rash in the damp of the low-lying estuary. Mostly, though, you'd hardly know it was there. Over at Mucking Marsh on the north side of the Thames, as at other sites, the vast disused landfill – once one of Europe's largest – is now capped and landscaped. In recent years its surface has been let to Essex Wildlife Trust, on what is known as a 'pie-crust lease', and apart from its rising unnaturally above surrounding marshland, there is little sign of the buried waste. Yet the nature reserve's award-winning visitor centre had to be built on a series of hydraulic jacks, to allow for the shifting and settlement of fifty years' worth of London's rubbish underneath.

In the distance a container ship appeared to pass over land, like something imagined. I stood up. It was almost high tide. Beneath the calls of waders, the water was rising without a sound. Still nothing seemed to have moved. Yet great swathes of mud had already disappeared, leaving islands of marsh stranded far from shore. The stereo was now lying in water. It was an odd sensation: rather than the basin filling from the sea, the water seemed to rise from the marsh itself.

In our estuaries in particular, the risks from our buried waste will come from rising seas and climate change, with increased erosion from storms and surges. As at Deadman's Island, in time the marsh will give up its buried secrets, amongst them this last century's poorly regulated landfill with all its unrecorded pollutants – from asbestos to the mercury and lead in batteries and electronics – because of course there is no 'away'.

Artificial plants found on Cornish beaches.

Obscure plastic animals found on beaches.

Tray of plastic finds, including two Lego dragons (1997)
and Smarties lids (1970s–2005).

Plastic dinosaur on a plastic landscape, with nurdles and microplastics. Found on one of Cornwall's 'collector' beaches which, following storms, are often covered with debris due to prevailing winds and quirks of local currents and geography.

Gradual breakdown of the flotsam army.

Plastic figure from the sea.

Plastic music-box ballerina.

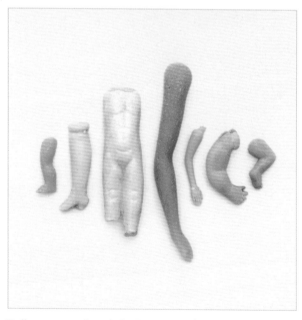

Doll parts: ceramic and plastic, nineteenth–twenty-first century.

Wheels from toy cars found on Cornish beaches over two winters.
The wheels wash ashore much more often than other parts, which
presumably break down more quickly or sink to the sea floor.

Plastic wise man. A French *fève*, traditionally hidden inside a *galette des rois* cake to celebrate the Epiphany. Originally fava beans, these were replaced by porcelain religious figures in the 1800s and 'collectible' plastic trinkets in the 1960s.

Shore finds, nineteenth–twenty-first century, including an iron musket ball (1800s), Pop-it beads, a roll-on deodorant ball, a Codd marble (1870s–1920s), golf ball innards, a bouncy ball and a 'floating widget', used in beer cans since 1997 and known by Guinness as the 'smoothifier'.

Soy sauce fish from takeaway sushi.

Headless horseman.

Party popper with the distinctive bite-marks of fish.

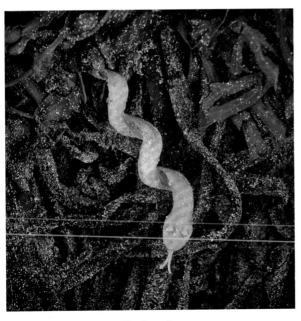

Plastic snake.

Plastic dog from the children's TV show *Sooty* that came free with Kellogg's Coco Pops in 1973.

Cassette tape: Britain's most popular music format, 1985–92.

Plastic bottle with goose barnacles. In the past the barnacles attached mainly to driftwood, but now they wash ashore on everything from plastic fishing gear to flip-flops and toothbrushes.

Toy soldier found on the strandline.

Plastic found on Cornish beaches, including a party popper, golf tees, hair-curler pins, a Smarties lid (1970s), a cotton-bud stick, biro lids, toothbrushes, guns, razors, a tiddlywink, a dummy, an obscure blue animal, pegs, an inhaler, Lego flippers lost at sea in a container spill in 1997 and a 'reward tag' from a shark tagged in the early 1970s (although by the time the tag was found in 2018, the reward 'pot' was empty).

Plastic found on Cornish beaches, including a Monopoly hotel, a single-use coffee pod, a Coca-Cola bottle top, golf tees, Fairy Liquid caps, biro lids, a bug from the 1980s game Bed Bugs, disposable lighters and a horseman with half a horse; also Lego flippers, spearguns and flowers from the 1997 container spill.

6

Isle of Sheppey

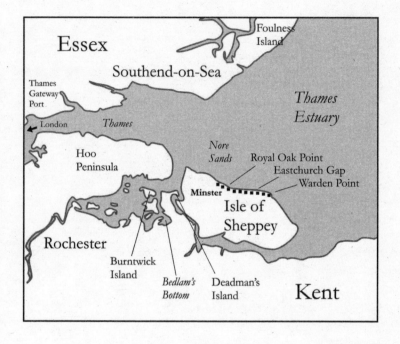

In October I headed back to where I grew up on the Isle of Sheppey. The island lies at the mouth of the Thames, and for centuries marked the entrance to that great highway of the British Empire, passed by London-bound sailing ships laden with tea, sugar and porcelain. The Nore sandbank – actually Great Nore and Little Nore – lies off Sheppey and at the time was a major anchorage for the English fleet. Its shallow waters provided an assembly point before naval battles with rival European colonial powers, as well as a stop-off before voyages to secure new trade routes. It also offered anchorage for the rising numbers of merchant sailing ships heading to and from London, from early schooners and galleons to the increasingly capacious East Indiamen – the ships' designs evolving steadily as the holds grew larger. Traces of the Thames's long history of maritime trade are sometimes recovered from the estuary floor, and include a sixteenth-century 'armed merchantman' found during dredging to deepen channels for the new London Gateway 'super-port'. Out on the estuary marshes, this deep-sea container terminal means the Thames is now capable of handling the vast new container ships I'd glimpsed from the marshes near Bottle Beach. Keeping pace with the scale of global trade, the true size of these ships is hard to grasp: giant cranes unload their thousands of HGV-sized containers, which from a distance look like no more than brightly coloured Lego.

The reason the Tolladays ended up on Sheppey is that by

the 1960s my grandad had saved enough extra money selling toot to buy a house there. Like many south Londoners, he and my nan knew the island from past seaside holidays. So when doctors told them he would soon need to leave the city due to the state of his lungs, they bought a small, light-construction bungalow at the edge of Minster village. In comparison to where they lived in London – where no one they knew owned their own home – houses and land on the island were cheap. So, during my mum's teenage years, they stayed at the bungalow at weekends and holidays, and at the age of eighteen she and my islander dad met at a dance in the local Working Men's Club.

By the mid 1960s they were married. With my grandparents yet to move to the island full time, my mum and dad rented the top rooms of their south London house. My dad was an electrician and, as this involved rewiring council flats, my grandad soon introduced him to the local toot shop (if he burnt the rubber off old electrical cabling, they would buy it for the copper). But living in London was expensive and my dad had a plan: they'd buy a cheap piece of land back on the island, build a house and live there 'just for a couple of years'. This was persuasion enough for my Londoner mum and they moved to Sheppey on the first day of the 1970s, with me a baby of six months – although in the end they stayed twenty-five years.

I drove back onto the island on a still afternoon, a couple of months after my trip to Bottle Beach. For nostalgia's sake I took the back road via the old Kingsferry Bridge, an odd 'vertical lift' bridge that, when I lived there, was the only way on and off the island. Since 2006, though, it has been in the shadow of a four-lane flyover. While this makes Sheppey feel less of an island, it does make for a more dramatic panorama as you speed down towards the marshes. Although wide-open and treeless in all directions, the horizon to the north and east – where most locals live – is crowded with distant industry, rooftops and trading estates. Yet to the south, beyond wild saltmarsh, the rest of the island is mainly farmland and reclaimed marsh.

Growing up on Sheppey, I don't recall ever wondering what outsiders thought of us. Recently, though, I'd found myself reminiscing about how, as a family, we'd go out beyond the sandbanks on low spring tides to collect old bottles. Making a connection between the bottles and London's barged-out rough stuff, I'd idly typed 'rough stuff Sheppey' into the Google search bar. First up was a review of a caravan site with the title 'Great if your into drugs and a chav'. Inevitably, this drew me in and I scrolled on through further searches to find a 'Let's Move To . . .' feature from the *Guardian*.

> If you don't like that landscape of smudgy, soggy marshland and vast skies common to the Thames Estuary, or the sewage works and paper mills that greet you on your arrival, look away now. What it has in spades, though, is that innate oddness and apartness peculiar to islands . . . Its landscape of prisons and marshes is not for everyone.

At that point, the only other mention of Sheppey I'd stumbled across in my research was a few lines in Peter Ackroyd's *Thames: Sacred River*: 'In 832 it was overrun "by the heathen men". It has not been the same since.'

The walk I'd arranged to do the next day, with my old school-friend Laurie, would start at the far end of the island. This is the end where holidaying Londoners have always stayed, where farms have run caravan sites since the 1950s and you can still buy cockles and whelks by the pint. A main attraction is the beach at Leysdown: although remote on the Sheppey marshes, it offers a strip of yellow sand an hour's drive from south London. As the timing of the tide was crucial for this walk, I would spend the night in the van and meet Laurie early the next morning. So I drove out along the edge of the marsh towards Warden, heading for a caravan site at the top of the cliffs.

I'd not been to the site before, but at last saw a sign and turned down a cracked and rutted lane. For some way there was no sign of a campsite and I began to wonder if I'd taken a wrong turn. I passed a house, then, set back from the lane on its own, with printed notices fixed to shut gates.

THESE DOGS WILL BITE
Trespassers will be shot

A few hundred yards on, I was directed past empty, out-of-season caravans to a deserted field overlooking the sea. A post-and-rail fence marked the edge of the crumbling cliff and out beyond it stood a row of abandoned electrical hook-ups.

Soon after arriving, I wandered back into Warden for a better look at what was left of the village. Reaching the main road I turned towards the sea, passing several houses before the lane began to narrow, as bushes crowded in at either side. A little further on, down the centre of the road, grass pushed up through ruptured tarmac. Then the road simply ended, its ragged edge jutting out into the air where the ground beneath had fallen away. I had imagined there would be some kind of barrier. But there was nothing: just the wide-open sea, slumping cliffs and the remains of fallen concrete buildings far below on the shore.

Once this was the road to Warden's church. An island legend tells of the church that 'went to the sea', which we often heard when we stayed with my dad's mum.

'On a still night', my nan would say, tucking me and my brother into bed, 'if you stand out on the cliffs you can hear the church bells toll beneath the sea.'

It was much later that I learned how the church was lost. One hundred and fifty years ago it stood at the edge of the cliff, closed and exposed to the weather. With parts already destroyed by high winds, it gradually became derelict, with locals eventually taking the pews and the pulpit for firewood. It was finally demolished in 1876 and what remained – mainly the graveyard and foundations – was left to go over the edge. Years later, local rumour told of an old woman who spent her days collecting the bones that washed out on the beach. Now, given the speed of erosion here, any remains would lie hundreds of yards offshore.

More recently I learned that this wasn't the first Warden church to be lost to erosion, as it replaced an older church that stood 'a mile or so further along the road'. So it's quite possible that the roots of the story my nan told (a legend common to many of Britain's eroding coasts) may lie in the loss of that earlier church.

I moved back from the bitten tarmac edge. When I was a child there were still houses here as well as a post office, which had previously been the Smack Aground Inn. Said to have taken its name from a group of local wreckers, by the early 1800s the pub was a base for a network of smugglers, the North Kent Gang. At the time, smugglers were referred to as 'owlers', not because they hooted to each other across the marshes – as I'd read somewhere – but from a corruption of the word *wool*, for as the first product subject to British export duties, it was the earliest contraband. With its remote beaches, and its name meaning 'island of sheep', Sheppey was a natural choice for those early smugglers, and remained so as they moved on to running tea, spirits and tobacco.

I first learned of the island's smugglers as a child, because one of the places my nan took us was the Love Lane burial ground, not far from where she lived. The highlight – and purpose – of these visits was our search for a particular head-stone, to read the inscription.

O EARTH
cover not my *BLOOD*
Sacred
to the Memory of
a MAN unknown, who was found
Murdered on the Morning of the 22nd
of April 1814, near Scrap Gate in
this Parish, by his Head being nearly
severed from his Body.

The story behind it was that the headstone had been paid for by a group of local smugglers – out of guilt, as while unloading on the beach one night, they'd mistaken a passing stranger for one of the government's 'preventive' men.

The next morning, Laurie and I parked in neighbouring Warden Bay, where the houses end, above a stretch of 'rock armour' brought in to protect the cliff against erosion. Below, the sea was flat calm, despite – or perhaps due to – the tail end of a hurricane forecast to arrive in a couple of days.

We set off along the stony beach, past gulls and oystercatchers strung out at the mud edge, waiting for the tide to fall. Offshore, odd shapes were just beginning to break the surface, appearing in silhouette against the low sun: a tyre and a concrete slab, the handlebars and front wheel of a bike. Presumably they'd all come down with the cliff, with the heaviest of the debris left stranded where it fell. As we headed towards Warden Point – which is no longer a point – the strange, unstable landscape felt almost immediately remote. On exposure to air, London clay weathers to brown, and here it rose above the shore in odd peaks and turrets. In places a crumbling, teetering pinnacle was held together by no more than the remains of a single scrubby bush, its exposed roots curling out into the air.

Although minor cliff-falls are common all along this stretch of coast, every now and then – with little or no warning – a major landslip will take acres of the cliff-top with it. This is more likely in the wetter months of winter or spring, but the process begins when the ground is dry, as the London clay shrinks and cracks open up. Later these fill with rainwater, which mixes with the clay to form a lubricant like potter's 'slip', leaving the cliff at risk of sheering internally. Sometimes, as the seaward section slips towards shore, its surface remains more or less undisturbed – perhaps just tilting gently inland. In 1870, the *Illustrated London News* described how an acre of 'Sheppey Isle'

> slipped from its original position, and the whole mass of earth glided with slow descent down the cliff to the beach, without even disturbing the surface of the ground . . . the wheat which was previously growing upon the land is still upright, and appears not to be in the least injured by the change of position.

There are other stories too: of corn being reaped halfway down the cliff; of people waking to find their garden or a neighbour's house has vanished; of a farmer finding nine of his sheep grazing unhurt on half an acre of pasture 100 feet below the cliff-top.

The reason for the instability is that the cliffs are continually seeking a more gradual natural incline, but as high tides repeatedly erode the base this is never achieved, meaning that the cliff-edge recedes by on average five feet a year. Given rising sea levels and the increase in storms and surges that will come with climate change, over the coming century the rate of loss is predicted to double.

That day, recent falls meant the beach was hard going. In places the shore was covered in slippery, fresh clay 'pebbles', making it almost impossible to walk on. So with the tide steadily revealing more of the foreshore, we headed out from the beach, favouring slick but hard beds of clay. I'd usually avoid these as being too slippery, but at least they were firm – which felt safer than the softer mud, which too often gripped my boot by the ankle as I sank. So I trailed after Laurie, with a cautious, flat-footed gait.

We stopped first at a place where metal collects. It was a spot I had searched in the past, and on a previous visit I'd turned up what I considered an extraordinary find. It was the grey of lead I noticed first, standing out amongst the rust-coloured pyrites, although it was only on picking it up that I realized it was a horse's head. I was delighted, as the legend everyone grows up with on the Isle of Sheppey is of Sir Robert de Shurland and his horse Grey Dolphin.

On school trips we would be taken to see his medieval tomb in the island's Minster Abbey, where Sir Robert's reclining effigy lies beside a horse's head emerging from the waves. As Baron of Sheppey, Sir Robert's rights included bloodwyte (the right to fine servants for the shedding of blood), childwyte (the right to fine the fathers of illegitimate children), and 'Wreck of the Sea', which entitled him to any wreckage found 'within the limits of his domain, whether ashore, "bumping" or even floating, within three miles of low-water mark'.

In order to claim the wreck as his, though, the Baron had to be able to touch it with the tip of his lance at low tide; so, to make the most of this, he is said to have trained his horses to swim. The best was Grey Dolphin, thought to be depicted by the horse's head carved into the tomb beside him.

The story we were told is that in the fourteenth century Sir Robert killed a monk. With the Church seeking retribution, the Baron heard that the King was anchored off Sheppey on the Nore sandbank, so saddled Grey Dolphin and swam out to his ship. He made a full confession and was pardoned by the King, then turned Grey Dolphin and swam back to shore. Although the exhausted horse managed to reach the beach at

Minster, a local witch was waiting. 'You think that horse has saved your life,' she told the Baron. 'But it will be the death of you.'

In response, he drew his sword and cut off the horse's head. A year later, though, he was walking that same stretch of shore when he injured his toe kicking what he thought was a rock. But it was the skull of Grey Dolphin. Within days Sir Robert's toe had festered and, back home at Shurland Hall, he died.

Standing on the shore holding the lead horse's head – actually the remains of a nineteenth-century child's toy – I swore quietly to myself at my luck. What were the chances of finding it where I had, on a beach little more than a mile from Shurland Hall? (At the age of twelve, a friend and I had camped alone in its isolated ruins, but got so scared we ran back to her house after dark.) A short time later, still flooded with treasure hunter's glee, I noticed a man making a detour towards me. He was in his twenties and carrying a rucksack. On reaching me, he said he was looking for sharks' teeth and showed me two he'd found.

'Any luck?' he asked.

I hesitated, before fishing in my pocket for the horse's head. I held it out to him.

He nodded. 'Nice.'

Suspecting he was about to reach out for it, I snatched my hand back – in a rush of fear that it was so precious he would be tempted to grab it and run. He glanced at me curiously as I stuffed it back in my pocket, before heading off to continue his search.

Today, at the same spot with Laurie, I found several modern coins – a grand total of eleven pence, and so salt-corroded I was initially hopeful they were older – and a bell. It was small and round, and although bent and damaged, it still had the pea inside. I rinsed it and gave it a shake, and although the sound wasn't exactly musical, it did – after a fashion – still ring. Later I learned it was a crotal bell: an animal bell dating to the seventeenth or eighteenth century. Known also as rumble bells, they were often attached to horses' harnesses to warn of approaching horse-drawn vehicles on quiet country lanes. On reflection, it seemed poignant to have found it where I did: where the old road once led out to the church, and the village and so much farmland has been lost to the sea. Presumably, it was also as close as I'd get to hearing church bells toll beneath the waves.

Despite feeling that we ought to press on, I made a detour out to the concrete ruins I'd glimpsed from the end of Warden Road. With Sheppey strategically located at the mouth of the Thames, the remains are of defensive positions used in both world wars – the most unusual being a First World War sound mirror, a giant concrete 'listening ear' that gave early warning of incoming enemy aircraft. Dominating the shore, though, were two Second World War pillboxes: shellproof bunkers that began to fall from the cliff in the late 1970s, but have survived the descent more or less intact. Now part-submerged except at low tide, they lay at crazy angles out on the foreshore, green with weed to well above head-height. Another had broken in two, and while half of it lay on the beach, the rest was still sunk in clay thirty feet up the cliff. I picked my way carefully amongst the remains of wave-worn slabs, out to the furthest of the pillboxes. Its doorway faced out to sea and, although entirely submerged at high tide, the water was low enough now to get out there.

As I waded out through the last few feet, silty water still poured from the doorway. Hanging back at the water's edge, Laurie described the eerie boom of the echo when the pillbox filled on an incoming tide – and then wandered off, saying she wasn't coming in because the weird angles made her seasick. As soon as I stepped up into the gloom, I saw what she meant. Everything felt wildly off-kilter. The back room was filled with water to the machine-gun slits beneath its concrete ceiling, and bars of amber sunlight lay on its murky surface – which appeared to slope madly uphill. I made my way carefully up sloping concrete, putting a hand to walls that were studded with barnacles, before emerging in a brighter second room. Here, the window holes faced up towards the cliff and sky. Slick piles of clay lay slumped against the walls, which above the high-water mark were scrawled with layers of graffiti. Although some of it looked relatively recent, most had faded to almost nothing. I wondered how much of it dated to the 1960s, when the pillboxes stood at the cliff-top surrounded by caravans.

After another mile or so we were able to walk more easily on the beach. The mudslides were still fresh, with the lowest plants so recently uprooted that their leaves hung wilted and greenish grey above the beach. As a child I knew these only as 'bog plants' and was warned to stay away from where they grew. Where the water pooled, the clay could be treacherous and we were always told that, if you got stuck, the more you struggled the faster you'd sink. When I was five years old, two boys from London were trapped in the mud overnight, and only one survived. So as children we were frequently warned of the danger and chose our routes up and down with care.

On his mum's side, my dad's family were all from the island and always lived near the cliffs. My nan played piano in the local pubs. As a teenager, she'd cleaned a woman's house in exchange for piano lessons and back at home drew black-and-white keys on the mangle in the yard to practise. On the pub-crawl coach trips they all called 'beanos', with no piano available, she played accordion, sometimes coming home covered in bruises as a result of the driver cornering too sharply. In the village pubs she played all the old cockney tunes and as a child I remember everyone standing round the piano singing.

Often, family and friends were associated with a particular tune, which she sometimes played when they walked in the pub door. For my dad's younger brother this was 'All the Nice Girls Love a Sailor'; their dad was a shipwright who specialized in masts, and my dad was the only brother who didn't work at the dockyard or go to sea. He did, though, always have a boat, even if most of his fishing stories seemed to involve getting stuck in the estuary mud at low tide (wearing weighty sewer boots my grandad had 'acquired') or waving a tilly lamp madly at night to avoid being run down by tankers. One memory my mum has is of him speaking proudly of a new boat he and a friend had built – and how, when my dad opened the van doors to show her, she was surprised to see 'what looked like a tin bath made of hardboard'. By the time they were married, my mum had her own song too, which – perhaps unsurprisingly – was 'My Old Man's a Dustman', with its memorable line about 'gorblimey trousers' (I wondered about this as a child, but imagine now that it had something to do with the string they tied round their ankles to stop rats running up them).

Having finally reached a firmer beach, it was a relief not having to watch so carefully where we trod. It also gave us more of a chance to take in our surroundings. Until then, I'd caught the occasional glimpse of fairly recent fly-tipped rubbish near the top of the cliff, and early on what appeared to be a distant fallen fridge. But it was only on reaching the sweep of stony shore at Eastchurch Gap that we began to find more eroding junk. With easy access by road, its bushy cliff-top has been a magnet for fly-tippers since at least the 1970s (and quite probably decades or centuries before that). At the time, house building was taking off on the island's cheap land, with a handy belief amongst local builders that dumping truckloads of rubbish over the edge would shore up the cliffs. In an image taken in the 1990s, a distant photographer has captured a vast trail of their rubble making its slow way down through the Hen's Brook valley to the shore.

I headed up to the top of the beach. There, only heavy seas and the highest tides reach the cliff, so a storm beach was banked high on shore: a tangled heap of dry flotsam and pebbles, the bleached roots of fallen trees, plastic bottles and a threadbare carpet. It looked like it had been there all summer and the first of my finds were obvious: a big doll's leg, an enamel chamber pot and a huge plastic leaf, which I held out to Laurie.

'Cheese plant,' she said. She shook her head. 'They're indestructible. Why the fuck would anyone want a plastic cheese plant?'

There was also plenty more to furnish a house, or perhaps a caravan. Further down the shore lay a wet heap of what looked like orange curtain material, a coat hook and several chipped fragments from a pink bathroom suite.

At the foot of the cliff, not far from where I stood, the bulky remains of a video recorder were just beginning to emerge from the clay. A few more spring tides and this too would wash out onto the beach and break up. I wandered further down the stones to where some patterned lino had already washed free, along with an entire section of tiled bathroom wall. I had no idea how long any of these things had been entombed in the cliff, but both the lino and the tiles would have been fashionable in the 1960s and 1970s.

By then, my mum's generation – the baby boomers – had abandoned the old-fashioned notion that thrift was virtuous, and were embracing the new material culture. Attitudes towards consumption had shifted considerably, along with the meaning of the word itself. Deriving from the Latin verb *consumere*, in Victorian times 'consumption' had implied a 'using up' or exhaustion of matter – hence its use to describe the 'wasting disease' that killed Ellen and Jane Tolladay. Yet from the 1950s, the word had begun to shed that aspect of its meaning and be seen as more positive.

Manufacturers, though, did have their concerns – that at some point people would have bought all the things they needed: the washing machine, the electric oven, the television set, the new bathroom suite. And, if left to their own devices, it was likely that before returning to buy again they'd simply wait for the original to wear out. Yet due to recent advances within industry there was the potential to produce so much more.

The manufacturers' solution was planned obsolescence. The best-known early example was the 'Phoebus cartel', which involved light bulbs (I find plenty of their metal screw- and bayonet caps on the shore). Although the evidence only emerged decades later, it turned out that from the 1920s a worldwide group of major light-bulb manufacturers – including Philips, General Electric and Osram – colluded to make their bulbs more fragile, so they would burn out faster. Whereas in 1924 the industry standard for a bulb was 2,500 hours, by the 1940s they had it down to 1,000 hours. Strikingly, one early bulb – manufactured in 1901 and known as the Centennial Light – is still shining in a California fire station, following its 'one million hours party' in 2015.

By the 1960s, planned obsolescence had become entrenched in a variety of forms – some more subtle than others. As with the Phoebus cartel, manufacturers were increasingly experimenting with 'contrived durability', making parts of lower quality materials so they would break more quickly. Effectively, products could now be made with predetermined lifespans, a process sometimes known as 'death-dating'.

Equally effective was 'perceived' obsolescence, where faster replacement rates were encouraged by more frequent changes to a product's style, giving the impression that the earlier version was old-fashioned and outdated. While this had always driven seasonal and annual cycles in the fashion world, now it began to spread to other industries.

Car manufacturers are often credited with being the first to draw on it. The story goes that in 1920s America, General Motors was struggling to compete with Ford – in particular its Model T, or 'Tin Lizzie', which embodied the company's traditional engineering values of quality, reliability and durability. Initially, General Motors' competitive focus had been on technology and quality of engineering, yet that had failed to make an impact. So Ford continued to maintain its edge largely through economies of scale and policies, such as offering the Tin Lizzie in any colour 'so long as it is black'.

However, things began to change after General Motors hired two executives with experience in the fashion trade. On their advice, the company decided that it would be cheaper and more effective to compete with Ford through style and design. By changing the look of their cars more frequently, these would date more quickly, encouraging customers to trade in their old models sooner. For General Motors, this proved a huge success. The company went on to incorporate other marketing ideas from women's fashion, advertising and retail, and in time overtook Ford to become world leader. Their competitors, including Ford, could only follow suit. In 1955, one General Motors executive spoke more plainly of their intentions than any would today: 'Our big job is to hasten obsolescence. In 1934 the average car ownership span was five years: now it is two years. When it is one year we will have a perfect score.'

I had already picked up several spark plugs, the most recent catching my eye with its unusual shade of violet-pink. Over decades, I've found plenty of these along the beach where we were headed, and I imagine many date to my childhood, when there was always a series of wrecked cars on their way down the cliff. Back then there was less incentive to take MOT failures to a scrapyard, and people simply drove to the edge of the cliff, took the hand-brake off and pushed the car over. At first, the dumped cars didn't always fall far – sometimes just far enough for them to be out of sight from the top. From down on the beach, though, it was the staggered arrangement that struck me most: the way the cars' bright paintwork gradually merged with the cliff, with the lower cars already rusted and misshapen as they sank into the mud.

By the 1970s, through a combination of marketing and planned obsolescence, the car had become – in the words of the historian Daniel Boorstin – a 'visible and easily understood symbol of personal progress'. At the start of the twentieth century there were 8,000 cars on Britain's roads; by 1970 there were 15 million. Growing up, we all understood, as if instinctively, the meaning of a Ford Cortina, a 3-litre Capri or a new BMW. I've no idea what models the spark plugs came from, but along with the wheels and suspension springs lying out in the mud, they represented the end of the line. To make room for shinier, more impressive replacements, we now had to get rid of things as big and complex as cars.

In just a few decades, the various forms of planned obsolescence had unleashed a revolution. By shortening product lives, manufacturers had overcome their fears of overproduction. As it turned out, we could be persuaded to buy more – and more frequently – than anyone could previously have imagined. As Vance Packard noted in *The Waste Makers* in 1960: 'The way to end glut was to produce gluttons.' Outside the counter-culture, the unprecedented growth of those decades promised liberation and affluence for all. Earlier attitudes towards profligacy and waste were fast becoming old-fashioned. And like buying tea to support the British Empire, for this post-war generation their purchasing power had a new legitimacy. Through supporting economic growth and stability, a more comfortable life was not only of personal benefit but also good for the country.

It wasn't until after the halfway point that we began seeing trees on the beach. Strangest of all were those still standing at a natural angle. From a distance the trees appeared to be growing right down to the lower shore. Closer to, though, it soon became clear they were dead; against the shine of the mud, the remaining branches were blackened as if burnt. It seemed incredible that they'd stayed upright on their journey down the cliff, and remained standing despite regular immersion at high tide.

Many were festooned with seaweed and rags. Scraps of material fluttered from higher branches, while other bundles hung heavy and low – the frayed, waterlogged remnants of fishing rope, old bedspreads and clothes. One bundle had snagged between branches, trapped like a bird with outstretched wings. With a bit of investigation I identified some of its contents, which were strikingly similar to those I find entangled with sea fans on my local beach in Cornwall: the sagging waistband from a pair of boxer shorts, a wet stocking, the ribbed sleeve from a child's jumper.

As far as I could make out, when we reached the last of the stranded trees we were below Royal Oak Point (which, like Warden Point, is no longer a point). It takes its name from the pub that once stood at the top of the cliff, which in the early 1950s was one of the places my nan played piano. Originally an isolated farmhouse, by the mid nineteenth century it had a reputation as another of the island's smuggler pubs. The old name for this stretch of beach is Bugsby's Hole, and it's said to be where the smuggled goods were brought ashore (a 'hole' was a place where a boat could land, meaning 'Holes' were once common on the Thames). In the 1860s the Royal Oak had extensive 'pleasure gardens' leading out to the cliffs, but by the late 1950s all of that had gone – leaving the pub so close to the edge it was deemed unsafe. So it closed down and for some time afterwards a chalked notice stood outside, for anyone who'd walked out to the end of Oak Lane.

'Sorry,' it said. 'This ain't a pub no more.'

Two decades later, when we went there as children, everyone knew it as the Pub With No Beer. By then it was a derelict shell not far from the cliff-edge, with the ruined piano still in the bar and the Gents already partway to the beach. In the end, before going over the cliff, it was burnt to the ground, and when I spoke to my brother recently about our childhood visits, his most vivid memory was of sitting on its doorless outside toilet, looking out to sea.

Up ahead, Laurie had sat down on the stones for a smoke, and I wandered over to see what she'd found. The first thing she showed me was a Bakelite switch, imprinted with OFF and ON. It was gorgeous and I was horribly envious, in no doubt that it was even better than a chamber pot or a leaf from a life-size plastic cheese plant.

Tired from what had often been difficult going, and no longer needing to worry about the tide, we sat for a while surrounded by half-buried builders' rubble. The best piece was nearby, a beautifully sea-worn granite kerbstone – one of many I'd fancied taking home before, but which of course I couldn't carry (I have no doubt that if this beach was even remotely accessible, the kerbstones would all have disappeared long ago). As on previous occasions, I wondered idly if this one might have been part of George Ramuz's project in the early 1900s, when he bought up a thousand acres of land along the island's cliffs. After marking out the unmade roads with kerbstones, he divided the land into plots. These were then offered for sale, for people to build their own homes. With island land as cheap as it was, quite a few plots changed hands locally when someone lost at cards.

In 1903, a piece appeared in the *Daily Express* describing Ramuz's land as a 'semi-circle of grassy cliffs, swept by the breezes of the German Ocean'. After that, another 3,000 plots were sold to around 1,000 Londoners. In the 1950s though, the original deeds were destroyed in a house fire. So for decades afterwards, people often had no idea whether or not a plot had sold – a particular problem where the owners didn't live on the island. I first heard about this when my own family lived on the cliffs, as it was of brief concern to my parents.

We moved there when I was nine years old, and for a year we lived in a caravan while my dad and others built a house. At the time, the cliffs behind the garden were still wild and un-defended, and I remember sitting on the slumped grassy ledges, looking out to sea and wishing I could be ten forever. Somehow, that memory is tied up with the work on sea defences, which began soon after we moved there. Although the local roads had remained unmade, an increasing number of houses were being built on Ramuz's plots. As a result the value of property at risk of erosion was rising. The cliffs were also lower than those at Eastchurch and Warden, which made the defence work less expensive. The outcome was that within a year of our moving in, they began draining the cliffs behind our house and levelling them to a more 'optimum' slope. Down on the shore, a concrete promenade and sea wall were also put in, along with a beach of imported stones. So almost as soon as we'd moved there, my strange, wild landscape had entirely vanished. To me at ten, unconcerned about the value of a house, this was a terrible loss – much like the idea of having to grow up.

One morning a few years later my mum looked out of the kitchen window to see a group of people fencing off the strip of cliff behind our garden. When she went out to ask what they were doing, they handed her a piece of paper, found when someone's great-aunt from London had died. Signed by George Ramuz, it was the original deeds confirming purchase of a 100-foot strip of land along the top of the cliff. Yet it wasn't long before the fence was pulled down, as it turned out that the great-aunt's plot – purchased in the early 1900s – had already been lost to the sea.

Other rubble I've regretted not being able to carry back includes wave-worn sections of brick wall. I've always loved them. Some are furred with weed, others scoured smooth by the tide and stones. On some the mortar wears fastest, and on others the brick – creating shallow depressions in which the retreating tide leaves collections of pebbles. Once, I did lug back a chunk of mortar and stone, as it was studded with worn fragments of coloured glass and tropical shells. Although I had no idea what it was, I liked the incongruity of finding decorative tropical shells in the estuary mud. Presumably this too came down the cliff with the tonnes of builders' rubble, as house building escalated into the boom years of the 1980s.

By then, local builders were buying up many of Ramuz's plots. House prices were rising and more and more people now aspired to own their own home. This was politically popular at the time, especially amongst Conservatives (not least because home owners were considered more likely to vote Conservative). It also put the home at the centre of the new consumer boom, amid a growing enthusiasm for home improvements. Down on the shore, the curling lino and chipped fragments of bathroom sink stood testament to this decade of new homes, DIY and extensions, of things pulled down, ripped out and replaced.

The 1980s was also the decade that brought easy credit with deregulation of the banks, which gave fresh energy to the boom. Like earlier shifts in attitudes towards consumption, debt too was now seen less negatively. With credit cards, we could all aspire. Galvanized by a surge in lifestyle advertising, we learned that our purchases could express not just status but also our identity. Crucially, the advertising industry was now attracting a wealth of creativity and bright new talent, all of it devoted to persuading us to buy.

As the decade wore on, the images on our television screens became richer and glossier, introducing us to glamorous lifestyles and guiltless indulgence, conspicuous extravagance and luxury brands. Later, as the 'trickle-down' of designer brands reached the island, we too came to recognize Gucci bags and Rolex watches, Ellesse trainers and Pringle jumpers (this happened just as my brother hit teenagerhood, so my mum would cut the logos off second-hand designer jumpers and sew them onto tops she bought him from the market). By the late 1980s, things considered luxuries at the start of the decade were fast becoming seen as essentials.

In the south-east, at least, the decade's stereotype was the yuppie with a fat City bonus, personifying the shift in attitudes towards excessive consumption. Before leaving Cornwall, I'd noticed a connection between those bonuses and the term my grandad used for the profit he made from the toot: his 'bunce' money. To begin with, I'd looked up the word *bunce* in several modern slang dictionaries, and every one described it as Cockney rhyming slang – short for 'Bunsen burner', meaning earner. Unconvinced that my grandad would have been using a word that had evolved from Bunsen burner, I looked it up to find that Robert Bunsen invented his burner in 1855. Yet in 1851 Henry Mayhew describes 'bunts' as already in common usage amongst London's costermongers, and a slang dictionary from 1859 describes it as 'costermongers' perquisites, the money obtained by giving light weight, &c . . . probably a corruption of bonus'. So it seems a Cockney somewhere worked creatively backwards for the rhyme with Bunsen burner.

By the 1980s, 'bunce' was back, used to describe the City bonuses. In the decade's climate of financial excess, old taboos against talking about money and wealth were falling away fast. One result was an explosion of slang expressions for money, with many revived from earlier decades and centuries. As well as bunce, the old 'spondoolicks' – from the money shells – was back, along with 'dosh', 'lolly', 'wonga', 'loot' and 'a wodge', each with its own colourful history (the roots of 'wonga', for example, lie in the Romany word for coal).

Some of these were expressions my dad used for his rolls of cash in the pub. In the mid seventies, he'd been made redundant by the Electricity Board and as a result 'went out on his own', doing maintenance work for supermarkets. To my outsider mum it seemed half the island was now self-employed. For my dad – along with some of the local builders – it worked out well. By the mid 1980s he was voting for Margaret Thatcher, had a jacuzzi and a brick-sized car phone, and drove a tip-up truck and a Porsche. At home, along with the Betamax video recorder, we now had more than one television set, an elaborate stacking stereo system, a 'ghetto blaster', a Walkman, a microwave oven, clock radios, an answering machine, Atari video games, even a 'grinder' beneath the kitchen sink (a waste-disposal unit that mangled dropped teaspoons in a similar way to the dustcarts). To us, all these things – must-have products we'd seen advertised on television – felt fashionable and new, and there was no sense they would ever be seen as outdated.

We walked the last stretch with the tide pressing stealthily ashore. Within sight of the smooth gradient of the cliffs where I'd grown up, I made a last detour to a couple of 'rockpools': one at the centre of a mud-sealed tractor tyre and the other – shallow but inhabited – in a half-buried but still zipped-up raincoat. Shouldering the rucksack, I suddenly felt incredibly tired. There was just so much waste. Yet, like today, when this was all being dumped, fly-tipped rubbish represented only a fraction of all the stuff passing through our lives.

In the 1980s, for the very first time in history, we began using more resources annually than the earth could replenish in a year – and the mood was celebratory. As the early plastics developers had proposed, it seemed we had truly broken free from the limits of nature. Then, in 1988, the earth had the hottest year on record (a year that now doesn't even make the top twenty, with the top five places taken by the last five years), and a wider public first began hearing that the dramatic rise in our consumption appeared to have costs and limits after all – it had just taken us a while to see them.

By the end of the decade, a consensus was beginning to form amongst scientists, of a long-term warming of the earth's climate likely caused by our burning of fossil fuels. They said the solution lay in reducing carbon emissions and switching to renewable sources of energy, and emphasized the need to act promptly. And, for the first time, concern spread from scientific and environmental communities out into the mainstream media and public awareness.

Among the first to see its full implications, specifically the potential impact on future profits, were the fossil-fuel industries. Exxon, for example, one of the world's largest oil companies, had been aware of climate change from at least 1981. And for a number of years, having assembled a team of in-house climate scientists and modellers, it was at the forefront of research into what at the time was known as the 'greenhouse effect', while remaining cautious about what it told shareholders. Towards the end of the 1980s, though, amid fears of potential govern-ment regulation of greenhouse-gas emissions, alarm bells began to ring. Exxon's research was cut back and the company instead began financing efforts to cast doubt on the science. One strategy was to help found the Global Climate Coalition, an international lobbyist group of businesses, with the aim of opposing any action to reduce emissions. Later, shareholder money would also be channelled into the work of climate 'contrarians' such as Willie Soon, whose research was almost entirely funded by the energy industry – to the tune of $1.2 million. It was clear to the industry that an atmosphere of public confusion would make it far easier to fight any attempts at government regulation. (In doing so, the fossil-fuel industry is often compared to the tobacco industry, which for decades successfully undermined scientists' findings that cigarettes cause cancer.)

The approach was quick to spread, with growing concern that any curbs on carbon emissions would affect profits well beyond the fossil-fuel industry. By the end of the 1980s, the subject had already become deeply politicized, especially in the United States, with conservatives and free-market think tanks promoting the idea of a 'global-warming conspiracy'. In the new era of deregulated capitalism, it became the environment versus the economy. The right claimed variously that the scientists were either lying or misguided, that changes were part of a natural cycle and human activity not a factor, and that the threat was a political hoax dreamt up by liberals and communists – which was met with a hysterical reaction from fanatical environmentalists. The outcome was everything that the fossil-fuel industry could have hoped: by the 1990s, the issue of climate change was engulfed in a paralysing fog of uncertainty.

Back at the campsite later that evening, my van was still the only one in the field. As it grew dark I sat in a foldout chair with a beer, beyond the reach of the orange glow from the rows of static caravans. I'd just rinsed out the mug and was flinging the dregs in a satisfying arc when a security guard emerged from between caravans and headed my way.

'Alright,' he said as he reached me. He stopped and chatted for a bit about the site, pointing out where a path had once run down to the beach. Four years ago, he told me, the cliff-edge was fifty feet further out.

'It went suddenly,' he said, looking out at the line of old hook-ups. 'But don't worry.' He paused at the sound of dogs turning nasty in the distance. 'You'll be fine tonight.'

Later, lying in the darkened van, I picked up my phone to listen to the radio before falling asleep, but instead clicked through to Google Earth. After scrolling along the island's cliffs, I followed the edge of the estuary back towards the marshes I'd visited in the summer. I'd done this repeatedly since the trip to Bottle Beach, and it had become almost reflexive. Although different in so many ways, there were similarities between the island's eroding cliffs and the drowning saltmarsh. Having spent my formative years by the estuary, I'm always drawn to its half-wild edges, where the land is too unstable to be turned into suburbs and the water is no longer the river but not yet the sea – and which of course will be among the first places lost to rising seas.

In the months between the two walks I'd pored over maritime charts of the estuary between Sheppey and Bottle Beach, tracing a landscape that resembled a jigsaw missing most of its pieces. Much of it was coloured green on the chart, indicating that for now it belonged neither to the land nor the sea. Fittingly, once out past Deadman's Island, there was a dark marsh-poetry to the names: Flats and Oozes, Slaughterhouse Point, The Shade, Slayhills, the Hopes and Blackslump Creek.

From the charts I'd moved on to Google Earth's satellite and aerial photographs, hoping that between those and the chart I could trace something of the history of the sea's encroachment over recent centuries. The marshes are lost during high tides and storm surges, as currents reverse in the creeks and water pours off the land, scouring the creek-banks and taking the mud with it. This process was clearly visible in the aerial photographs, where khaki streaks swirled from the mouths of creeks, pouring through bottlenecks between islands and out into wide main channels.

It was in this way that the pastures out beyond Bedlam's Bottom had eroded over the centuries, where once they stretched for three miles to the main shipping channel. To begin with, as the creeks continued to widen, broad tracts of marsh began to separate. Eventually, these were reduced to islands stranded out in the estuary, connected in the end by 'strayways': narrow ridges of higher ground trailing out across mudflats. As the last land bridges leading out to marsh pastures, these were shored-up for decades by the dumping of London's rough stuff, until finally they breached during North Sea surges.

Today the outermost of the three islands is Burntwick, which in the 1700s was the first to separate from the mainland. For another century and a half it was periodically inhabited – at one time by the same North Kent Gang of smugglers who drank at Warden's Smack Aground Inn, and later by a shepherd and his wife. Finally, before this low-lying island was abandoned, it was used as yet another dumping ground for London's barged-out waste, and by the army as a barracks and torpedo school in the Second World War. Traces of that time are gradually eroding away, but on a high spring tide kayakers sometimes film themselves paddling over the drowned island and in through the windows of the derelict barracks building.

The very last of the strayways – which in living memory ran out to Slayhills on the middle island – was a narrow track once known as the Sea Road. Although this breached for good in the notorious 1953 floods, which devastated places all along Britain's North Sea coast, this island was also not immediately abandoned. For years it was still used to graze sheep, and somewhere out in the mud lie the remains of a low barge that ferried them out there.

When I first saw the islands on Google Earth, they looked very different to the mainland marsh. It was a while before I understood why, but when I did the realization was sweet: the plane had passed over at high tide and in the stitched-together photographs, the islands lay just beneath the surface of the water. Semi-submerged in this way, they were strikingly beautiful. Neither the colour of the land nor of the sea, the drowned saltmarsh was rich, unexpected half-colours. Rather than the green of the charts, it had taken on violets and deep midnight blues, and in places indigo, where I imagined the water was deepest. From above, the complex, meandering pattern of the creeks and gullies was also revealed, dividing and subdividing into ever more intricate networks that drained the land like capillaries reaching every part of a body. At their edges the islands began to fray, fading away to dissolve into the colours of the estuary. (More recently, I returned to the images to find Google had updated them; this time the plane had passed over at low tide and everything was the brown of mudflats.)

That night, though, lying on the van's pull-out bed, I scrolled around the jewel-coloured islands looking for traces left by humans; for the remains of structures where successive generations had tried to hold back the tide. On Burntwick, the unnatural straight lines of drainage dykes cut across sinuous creeks, and the ridges of breached sea walls stood out in open water. I scrolled on, over neighbouring islands and fingers of saltmarsh, all with the same branching channels and drowning colours. Zooming in, the detail was extraordinary. I traced the outlines of sunken barges and more abandoned sea defences, picked out the pale cockleshell beach at Coffin Bay on Deadman's Island. Just as stark were the remains of the strayways, reaching bony fingers out into the estuary, pointing to patches of marsh that were now underwater.

In the dark of the van, it felt like a glimpse of the future. For as climate change brings rising seas and increased storms and surges, this is how the land will be lost. And it is all closely linked to those vast container ships, which pass like spectres out at the horizon and over the estuary marshes – veiling the true scale of our wastefulness and insatiable consumption.

PART III

The Sea

7

Penhale, North Cornwall

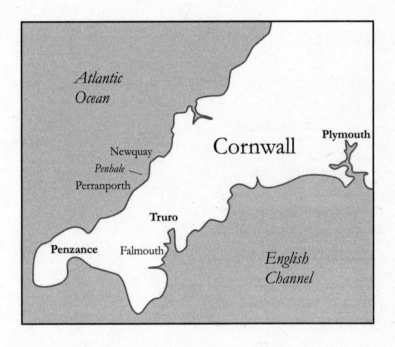

Atlantic Ocean

Newquay
Penhale
Perranporth

Truro

Penzance Falmouth

Cornwall

Plymouth

English Channel

Back in Cornwall that December, after a morning school run I set off for the north coast. It was raining hard and barely light, and beyond winter hedges the fields were dissolved in a murky gloom. I was going despite the weather, as after several days of gale-force westerlies, the beachcombing was likely to be good. Yet turning up onto the A30 at Bodmin, heading west along the county's granite spine, I'd still not settled on which of several beaches to try. For there are many 'collector beaches' in Cornwall, where prevailing winds and quirks of local currents and geography mean that after storms they're often covered with debris. This is rubbish that in one way or another has escaped the waste stream, and for most of the time remains hidden from sight – either drifting at sea or buried in sand. In Cornwall, many of these bays are sandy and idyllic, some windswept and remote, and ten or fifteen years ago it was a shock to see them littered with debris. Now, though, it is depressingly familiar to find them strewn with plastic: the material that has come to define this stage in the evolution of our waste.

Yet I can never be sure of what I'll find until I get there. On these wilder coastal shores, the fickle, conjuring tide can be far more dramatic than on the tidal Thames. While covering a beach in debris one day, it might clear it completely the next, spiriting everything away as if it was never there. That morning, if I did find much on the shore, I had no doubt that amongst it would be the usual, everyday objects that reflect our modern addictions to convenience, novelty and ease, and which have brought us to the point where our waste now threatens to overwhelm us. For me, the discord in finding these everyday objects so out of place on a beach can be particularly revealing, as in our own lives those same things are so familiar they've become invisible.

I slowed down as the rain intensified, scudding up the windscreen and hitting the roof like handfuls of flung grit. I flicked the wipers to high speed but could still barely see. Cars and trucks overtook me, their red taillights streaking past to vanish in spray; as an articulated lorry thundered by I gripped the wheel as everything turned white. When the road reappeared it shone like a river.

By then I'd settled on a beach near Perranporth, but almost missed the sign. Ten minutes later, turning off for a caravan park in the dunes, I was relieved to see the rain easing off. As usual I was struck by the peculiarity of the landscape, in part as there was no sign yet of the sea. These dunes are the highest in Britain and stretch for two and a half miles along this exposed Atlantic shore, rising in odd, irregular peaks long stabilized by grass and low scrub. In the distance, a sprawl of dun-coloured caravans hunkered down amongst them. I headed that way, past gnarled gorse trunks that snaked along the ground – stunted by harsh onshore winds – then empty caravans and a deserted holiday village of closed cafes and plank-fronted surf bars. Eventually, out beyond the last of the caravans, I pulled up at the sloping edge of a flooded car park. Outside the cocooned warmth of the car there was now just a trace of rain in the wind. I set off through the dunes along sandy paths, which crossed and divided to leave no obvious route to the sea. Although I'd been many times before, wherever the track forked I still found myself glancing back to check where I'd come from, trying to memorize the route back to the car. In a few high places, stakes had been driven into the sand, presumably to give those returning to caravans something to aim for.

I crested a dune and all at once faced the wide-open sweep of the bay. The sea's roar was constant, with gale-driven waves breaking in concert right out to the horizon. Their torn white crests arced out against the dark of the sky, yet it was only when they crashed up over distant headlands that there was any real sense of their epic scale.

I scrambled down a last sheer slope where the dune ended in a sand cliff, the rest having washed away in the storm. Down on the shore, it was hard to take it all in. In both directions, for as far as I could see, the beach was littered with plastic. Higher up it was tangled amongst seaweed, with the rest of the gently shelving shore covered with swathes of bright-coloured fragments. It was worse than I'd seen it before. Yet my initial feeling was a familiar, uneasy ambivalence: dismay at what we'd done to the oceans, along with a thrill at the things I might find.

I set out along the highest of the strandlines, head down and intent, so as not to be overwhelmed. Finds on Cornwall's Atlantic shores can be quite different to those on its more sheltered English Channel beaches, and one of the first things I picked up was a yellowed plastic bottle embossed with Spanish writing. Although most of the words were obscured by the intricate white doodles of keelworm tubes, I could make out the words *concentrada* – concentrated – and in larger letters *Peligro*, danger. The contents were long-gone and it looked to have been in the water for years. On these northern beaches it's not uncommon to find Spanish writing on the washed-up plastic and – like other things I'd found here and traced in the past – some may well have hitched a ride on the North Atlantic Drift, an extension of the Gulf Stream. These currents run like great rivers through the oceans, drawing warmer waters up from the Gulf of Mexico and along the east coast of America, before crossing some 3,000 miles of open Atlantic. It was these same currents that in the days of sail had dictated the triangular routes of the slave trade. There was no doubt that amongst today's washed-up plastic, some would have taken a similar route to those slave ships returning from Caribbean plantations laden with sugar, cotton and tobacco.

The Gulf Stream is also the reason that for thousands of years, parts of northern Europe have been much warmer than other regions at similar latitudes (Newfoundland in Canada, for example, has pack ice in its seas). However, research suggests that among the far-reaching effects of climate change will be a slowdown in these currents. As part of the North Atlantic Gyre – a system of currents circling the calm of the vast Sargasso Sea – any changes have the potential to alter weather patterns not just in Europe but also globally (and, of course, it is those same currents that bring the eel larvae to Europe and allow the silver eels to return to their distant spawning grounds).

For most of us, it's only in recent decades that we've become aware of these great ocean gyres, largely because their rotational currents create a vortex that draws in floating debris. Of the five major gyres in the world's oceans (circling clockwise in the northern hemisphere and anticlockwise in the southern), the first to enter public awareness was in the North Pacific. In the late 1990s, newspaper reports described researchers coming across 'an island of floating trash the size of Texas', dubbing it the Great Pacific Garbage Patch. Although this description has since proved misleading – today it is more often described as a 'plastic soup' – it created a powerful image that captured our attention. It was a shock: to have had no idea it was out there, in a place so remote from land and sources of pollution that we'd imagined it pristine. Yet once researchers began to look, it turned out that similar concentrations of plastic debris were trapped at the centre of the other major gyres, too – including a vast North Atlantic Garbage Patch in the Sargasso Sea.

I wondered if my ragged plastic bottle might have skirted the gyre. Where had its journey begun? How long had it been adrift? Was it drawn towards that plastic soup by the currents but let go? I will of course never know, but just occasionally something washes ashore that is traceable – as with a buoy I'd found recently on a nearby beach.

It was tangled amongst weed on the strandline and had the word WIZARD hand-carved into its hard, worn polystyrene. When I picked it up it was heavy with goose barnacles, which hung from what at sea would have been the underside. Although in a pre-plastic age these barnacles attached mainly to driftwood, I've found them on everything from washed-up flip-flops and plastic bottles to toothbrushes. These strange creatures spend their lives on the open ocean, and are named for the medieval belief that they were the embryonic form of the barnacle goose (as the birds migrate to breed, no one in Britain had ever seen their eggs). As larvae, goose barnacles drift in the plankton until chancing on flotsam, at which point they cement themselves on, growing shells at the end of long rubbery 'goose-necks'. Their size can be a clue to how long flotsam has been adrift, and on occasion they can provide forensic evidence: in 2008, when mature colonies were found on several suitcase-sized bundles of cocaine that washed up on Cornish beaches, it suggested they may have drifted from the Caribbean.

As WIZARD was probably the name of the boat the buoy had come from, I took it home to see what else I could find out. Given the currents of the Gulf Stream, much of the fishing gear washing up on these beaches originated on the east coast of America – so first I looked up US-registered boats for one named *Wizard*. It turned out there were a lot. So I posted a photograph of the buoy in several places online, on the off-chance it might be recognized. The best response was from a Facebook group called 'All Things Lobstering', with an early suggestion that it could be from the Alaskan crab boat *Wizard*, made famous in the TV documentary series *Deadliest Catch* (others in the group felt this unlikely due to currents and the size of the buoy). Then later that day I had a message from a member named Joe, saying he thought he recognized the buoy: it could be from a lobster boat out of Point Pleasant, New Jersey, some thirty miles south of New York. When I next heard from Joe, he'd texted the photograph to the owner of *Wizard* – the Point Pleasant lobsterman – who'd said yes, the buoy was one of his. But it was eight years since he'd last cut the boat's name into any of his buoys; these days he burnt it in. From my photograph, he was sure this one had been out in the Atlantic 'for every bit eight years'. It wasn't the most attractive buoy I'd ever found, but knowing where it had come from changed things. I kept it and wondered on and off about its journey, while it hung drying in the garden, its dangling barnacles very gradually losing their fishy smell of decay. (When the children were small we were once many miles from home when they smelt something odd. 'Eugh,' my son said quietly to his sister, 'you can smell Mum's fish from here.')

The wind had picked up and I crouched with my back to it, freeing a glow-stick from a tangle of weed. At home I have quite a few of these. They are the kind that were common at raves in the 1990s: when the plastic stick is bent, a glass ampoule inside is broken, triggering a chemical reaction that makes it glow. For years I'd found it strange to find so many on Cornish beaches, imagining at first that they came from surfers' beach parties. It turned out they were actually lost fishing gear: as fish such as tuna are attracted to light, the sticks are used as lures, strung by the hundred from long-lines and nets, and inevitably lost.

Ahead, a tangled heap of fishing net and rope lay stranded partway up the beach. There were other bundles in the distance, too, bright with synthetic oranges and blues but heavy as beached corpses. At sea, lost or abandoned nets can act as 'ghost gear', drifting beneath the surface like deadly curtains, trapping fish, seabirds and marine mammals. Every year an estimated 640,000 tonnes of fishing gear is left in our oceans, with the problem made worse by the fact that almost all of it is now synthetic. Until the 1950s, fishing nets were made from biodegradable materials such as hemp or sisal, whereas today 95 per cent of the lost gear is plastic. Durable and cheap, the new materials like PVC and nylon proved ideal for the extreme conditions at sea. As with so many other products, the shift to plastics also brought prices down, reducing the cost of replacement, so that abandoning a net became an easier decision. The problem is that these synthetic materials don't biodegrade, so for decades and centuries to come they will go on harming and killing wildlife in all sorts of horrific ways.

I picked up another plastic bottle, this one ragged with what looked like the bite-marks of fish (some species have strikingly sharp jaws). It reminded me of another a friend found here recently, its thick green plastic pierced by the distinctive diamond-shaped bite-marks of a turtle. I dropped my own bitten bottle in the bag to take home. Despite the lethal nature of abandoned fishing gear, it is these familiar household items – the things we all buy – that feel most telling.

After another couple of hours' searching I straightened up at last, stiff from crouching and looking. The tide was way out now but the wind-blown spray hung in the air, drawing a gauzy veil over the distant beach. Looking out along the debris-strewn shore, it was hard to imagine the force of the waves that had thrown it all up.

I spotted the white plastic lattice of a hair curler and dropped it in the bag, which was now almost full of plastic – not surprising, as plastic makes up by far the major part of all the rubbish that washes up on our beaches. Amongst it were golf tees and bottle caps, clothes pegs and combs, the remains of several plastic plants, biro lids, two toy soldiers and a plastic soy-sauce fish from takeaway sushi. As soon becomes apparent on these collector beaches, most of the plastic wasn't lost at sea but originated on land: it washes from gutters into sewers and storm drains, blows from roadsides and bins into rivers, and is swept from beaches by waves. Today's bagful was a fairly standard haul and, in our global world, beach cleaners everywhere find the same things.

Inevitably, therefore, it is the same familiar objects and their disintegrating fragments that turn up in the stomachs of marine animals, fish and seabirds. Some of the most haunting images of this began appearing over a decade ago in 2009, with Chris Jordan's series of photographs of the remains of Laysan albatrosses. Taken within a marine reserve on a remote Pacific atoll, the images were as shocking as the previous decade's 'islands' of floating trash. Each shows the remains of a single albatross, often a chick. The strongest images retain the birds' subtle, fading beauty: the airy bones, the curl of breast feathers, the archangel curve of a wing. Yet within each is a hard mess of coloured plastic, some scattered across the ground, some still held within the basket of a ribcage.

As on the beach today, most of that plastic is unrecognizable fragments. But as always it is the familiar, everyday objects that give the images their power: the bottle tops, lighters and pen lids; the toothbrush and cheap plastic toy. Skimmed from the surface of the ocean on foraging trips out to the Great Pacific Garbage Patch, the birds mistake plastic for the colourful squid and cuttlefish of their natural diet (it also appears that a coating of algae on the plastic releases an odour that triggers the birds' foraging behaviour). The majestic, legendary albatrosses then return to the atoll and feed the plastic to their chicks.

I picked up yet another Bic biro lid, this one so faded a blue I wondered how long it had been out there. Launched in 1950, when people were still refilling their pens with ink, Bic's cheap ballpoint was the pioneer of mass-produced disposable pens. Like so many innovations of the time, it proved more convenient than its predecessors at little or no extra cost. After pens, Bic – and long-term rival Gillette – then brought us disposable lighters and razors, several of which I'd also picked up. In removing the need for refilling and sharpening, these too made our lives just a fraction easier. Steadily, as cheap, disposable products became ever more prevalent, we discovered more needs we didn't know we had. In time, as we grew used to new ideals of comfort and convenience, we took to everything from disposable cutlery, coffee cups and plates to Styrofoam takeaway boxes and single-use nappies (although we did draw the line at disposable Bic underwear). So long as the waste was soon whisked from sight, it turned out we could overlook a great deal for the sake of convenience.

As we grew comfortable with disposability, both the products and materials began to lose their value, and it wasn't long before plastic was given away free. Cheap plastic toys had arrived with the advances in injection moulding, and in Britain some of the earliest freebies came with boxes of cereal. Kellogg's was at the forefront of this marketing revolution, something I discovered after finding a washed-up cycle reflector in the shape of their cockerel logo. Back home, following a trail of internet searches, I learned it was one of six 'collectible' cycle reflectors that came free with boxes of Kellogg's Corn Flakes in 1989.

This discovery led me off into a world of vintage toy collectors. I came across lovingly compiled websites with detailed descriptions of over seventy years' worth of British cereal-box toys, listing every colour and member of a set. I found hundreds for sale on eBay – some played with, others 'mint in package' – and wondered about the people who'd saved them unopened for decades. Particularly collectible was the pioneering frogman diver that came free with Kellogg's Corn Flakes in 1957. With baking powder packed in the foot, when submerged in the bath it would rise to the surface powered by bubbles. It is said to have been wildly popular, which was confirmed by the reaction I got on mentioning it to several friends in their seventies.

Inspired by the success of the diver, Kellogg's competitors soon followed suit. I scrolled on through decades of cereal toys, through a mind-boggling array of plastic – from 'Stretch Pets' and novelty torches to Coco Pops 'spoon toppers', plastic pan pipes and Batman periscopes. On learning that these freebie toys were produced in the tens of billions, I began wondering if any more of my beachcombed finds might have been fished from cereal boxes.

Most of the toys were in my trays of best finds. They lay alongside each other in separate wooden compartments, sorted by type. Methodically, I passed over the robed priest, the Viking and the parachute men, half a cherub and the painfully thin ballerina – the kind that pirouettes when you open a music box. I discounted the tiny bow-legged cowboys and Indians, the knights, the headless horseman and all the plastic soldiers. These are common finds and have rarely fared well at sea. Along with weapons bent out of shape, many of the figures were missing arms and legs, sometimes heads, and a couple were sliced cleanly through at the waist. Others were no more than wave-worn torsos, or stands with just the knobs of feet. I recognized none from the cereal toy website.

After that I sorted through the plastic animals, amongst them a kangaroo, a rat and a running hare, half a dog, several goats, a tiny pig, a glow-in-the-dark spider and a plastic T-Rex on a plastic landscape – again none familiar from the site. Of all the animals, my favourites are the most obscure. Faded and abraded after years at sea, tails and ears have worn away to nothing and some have only stumps for legs. The best are so worn they have the look of transitional species: a wildebeest-sheep, a stegosaurus–anteater, a hellhound–leopard.

Then a creature I'd always thought of as an orange bear caught my eye, because something in its raised arms looked familiar. So I took it to the computer and began scrolling back through the lists of cereal toys. Minutes later, there it was on the screen: it turned out it wasn't a bear but a glove-puppet dog – Butch, from the children's TV show *Sooty*, which first aired in the 1950s. And this particular series of Kellogg's cereal toys – 'Sooty and Friends' – came free with boxes of Coco Pops in 1973. I compared it to the row of 'mint' toys on the website, which were a shiny orange. After forty-five years at sea or buried in sand, my own Butch had faded and his teeth had worn away; along with ragged ears, he also had welts and dirty knees.

I was delighted, though, to learn what he was. These give-aways were an early example of TV merchandising, a strategy that reached new heights with blockbuster movies (if I show my trays of beach finds to children, it's usually the recent Minion they touch first). At the time Butch was fished from his cereal box, brands were increasingly recognizing the effectiveness of targeting children – not only for the more immediate rewards of pester power, but also as a longer-term way of influencing the next generation. By embedding habits such as brand aware-ness and impulse buying early on, there was a good chance they would stay with people through life.

In the decades since the heyday of the cereal-box toy, cheap, disposable plastic has reached into every corner of our lives, in ways no one then could possibly have imagined. On Cornwall's beaches, I find everything from plastic spoons and party poppers to the array of flushed plastic that makes its way from our bathrooms to the ocean: cotton-bud sticks, tampon applicators, packaging from medicines and pills, little plastic tools for flossing teeth. Which means that it's often on the beach that I'm pulled up short and glimpse the extent of plastic in my own life – more than once, by the inner workings of a stick of deodorant.

Most recently, though, it was a lid, which was small and ribbed, one of the simple screw caps that used to come on all tubes of toothpaste. Seeing it lying on the sand made me realize how much toothpaste lids had changed in recent years. These ribbed lids are common beach finds and some are no doubt from the old metal tubes (which I also find on the Thames Estuary beaches, sometimes with the end still neatly folded to squeeze out the last of the toothpaste). As is so common with modern packaging, the more recent tubes have become increasingly complex, so that today's designs are made from multiple layers of different laminated materials. As with crisp packets – made from up to seven layers of foil and plastic – this can make recycling difficult or impossible. The most recent change is that the tube now comes with a huge plastic lid, so it can stand on its head, saving us the trouble of rolling the end to squeeze out the dregs.

It brought home to me how, despite my initial dismay at the shift to squeezable plastic sauce bottles with enormous 'top-down' lids, I'd begun to stop noticing their spread. In what seems no time at all, these bottles and their lids (described by the innovators as 'boldly oversized') have become as normal as the versions they replaced. As well as ketchups and sauces, my local supermarket now offers 'top-down, squeezy' mayonnaises, mustards, pickles, creams, honey and jam; and in time these are likely to be the only containers those products can be bought in – although it may take all of us a while longer to adjust to the new upside-down squeezy Marmite 'jar'. Such packaging changes are rarely sudden, with the new versions first offered alongside the old, for those who might resist.

Out beyond the waves and spray, the horizon had blurred through a veil of distant rain. There was no trace now of the vessel that was out there earlier, which even then was no more than the vaguest shape of a container ship. Even more so than on the Thames Estuary, from shore the container ships out on the horizon here have no sense of reality or scale, or of any connection to our own lives. This makes it hard to believe that this largely invisible industry now brings us close to 90 per cent of everything we buy. Some ships can transport 20,000 truck-sized containers at once, and a staggering half billion of them are now shipped around the globe every year – packed with everything from food and toys to televisions and cars. In a reflection of rising world consumption, the largest of these ships are now six times the size they were at the start of the 1980s.

Occasionally, the containers are lost overboard. In time, their contents often wash up on a beach somewhere, and today's storm-cast debris had provided its usual oddly random glimpse. One was a fragment of bright pink lid. At home I had others the same shade, all from the 'pink tide' of plastic bottles that began washing ashore in Cornwall in 2016. This was a striking sight, with vivid swathes of pink drifting offshore and left scattered on beaches. Although unlabelled, the brand's distinctive colour led to them being quickly recognized – ironically – as 'Vanish' stain remover. It wasn't long before the parent company confirmed that they were from a shipping container lost off Land's End eight months earlier. From the delay in the bottles washing ashore, it appeared that the container had sunk to the sea floor and only begun releasing its twenty-seven tonnes of stain remover once disturbed by winter storms.

No one knows how many containers are lost at sea, in part because it's not mandatory to report a loss – and of course no company wants its brand linked to ocean pollution. While some claim that 2,000 are lost every year, others believe it's closer to 10,000. It is usually during storms and heavy seas that they break free of their constraints, with some (particularly the more watertight refrigerated containers) drifting for a couple of months as they take on water and gradually sink. Given time, their contents will usually be liberated. If buoyant, many of these objects are likely to turn up on our beaches, eventually as unrecognizable fragments like those littering the sand today.

After the initial Vanish clean-ups in Cornwall, whole empty bottles and lids continued to wash ashore for over a year, although now it's mainly pink plastic shards and bits of lid.

It's rare, though, for the arrival of a container spill on Cornwall's beaches to be as dramatic as the waves of pink. More commonly, regular beachcombers simply notice something turning up with an odd regularity. In recent years, along with IV drip bags and distinctive white plastic Christmas decorations, the spill finds have included Hewlett Packard ink cartridges – lost during an Atlantic storm in 2014 – and Nestlé 'tea capsules'. As usual, there were already a couple of the latter at the bottom of my bag. Like the ink cartridges, the tea capsules are thought to have been lost in a container spill in 2014, this one in the Bay of Biscay. Although four years later the capsules' coloured foil has long since disintegrated, a piece of plug-sized black plastic remains. I'd been noticing these on local beaches for some time before a friend explained what they were: designed for Nestlé's 'premium-portioned capsule tea maker', each is used to make a single cup of tea. At the time, I had no idea that such a thing existed. It turned out to have been inspired by single-serve coffee pod systems, which among other things 'reduce the time needed to brew' and 'eliminate the need to measure out portions'. Given the extent of the waste they produce, the inventor of America's biggest-selling capsule has expressed regret, saying 'I feel bad sometimes that I ever did it'. But it's too late now. For once we've known a new level of convenience – however minor or trivial that might be – there seems to be no going back.

Plastic has of course transformed our lives, in many ways for the better. As well as an alternative to scarce natural materials, it has also, for example, reduced fuel consumption by lightening cars and made possible many life-saving medical advances, from pacemakers and intravenous drips to replacement knees. The problem is that we've misused it, through turning a valuable, non-renewable resource into disposable, single-use products. While the oil that plastic is made from took millions of years to form, we turn it into products that might be used for minutes before being discarded.

Today almost half of all the plastic we make is for single-use products. Amongst the scattered fragments at my feet, only a few were still recognizable: a bottle cap, an aerosol nozzle, the broken end of a takeaway fork. But it is all there, including the remains of all the myriad forms of plastic packaging – trays, bags, bottles, pouches and wraps – that allow food and drink to be shipped to us over thousands of miles. This single-use plastic has transformed the way we shop, making possible our transition from local customer to global consumer, reliant on the disposable packaging that the industry describes as 'one ways'.

With so little value placed on resources, an older industrial cycle – where materials were more likely to be reused or recycled – has been broken. And as long as it remains cheaper for manufacturers to source virgin plastic rather than recycled, they will continue to do so. Today, only a tiny 2 per cent of plastic packaging uses any recycled content at all. Instead, valuable and finite resources continue their one-way journey to landfill or incinerators, or escape into the environment and end up in our oceans.

While it is preferable to all of those outcomes, recycling is not the panacea we would like it to be. As well as the energy used in transport and processing, and technical limitations such as lower-quality materials produced by downcycling, our reliance on overseas recycling markets is particularly problematic. Until China's 2018 bans on imported waste, two-thirds of Britain's recyclable plastic was being shipped there. Since that market closed, without the necessary infrastructure in the UK, much is now piling up here or being shipped to other distant countries, such as Thailand, Malaysia and Vietnam. As the waste is often low grade, poorly sorted or contaminated, some of it inevitably ends up being dumped as landfill instead. When this happens in countries with poor records of waste management, there is also a fair chance of some of our waste ending up in their waterways and the ocean.

Another charge is that recycling can assuage our guilt, absolving us of the costs of our energy-hungry lifestyles. In the view of *New York Times* writer John Tierney, we embrace recycling as an act of moral redemption, 'a rite of atonement for the sin of excess'. Like that sweet, clean feeling of a drive to the tip or putting the bins out, recycling allows us to make room for more.

It had started to rain. I paused in my search to watch a herring gull jerk backwards from a tangled heap, trying to free what looked like the remains of a fish. I pulled up my hood and at the movement the gull took off, leaving whatever it was behind. Sweeping out across the sea – perhaps towards the bins of Newquay – it was strikingly white against the darkening sky.

I headed back towards the car, angled against the rain and gusting wind. My last finds were the ball from a roll-on deodorant and yet another piece of toothbrush. I looked back across the littered shore. The visible end-of-life debris of every one of these discarded items was just a tiny fraction of the waste generated throughout that product's lifetime, most of that before it even left the factory. For every bin bag or wheelie bin of rubbish we put out at the kerb, many more have been generated 'upstream' during the collection or creation of raw materials and manufacture.

This sea-worn piece of toothbrush, then, had a long history behind it – in more ways than one. It was attractively wave-worn: plain and flat with rows of holes where it was missing the bristles. It was the kind everyone used before the 1980s – a simple design that had barely changed since 1780, when William

Addis began manufacturing the first mass-produced toothbrushes made from bone. Although bamboo brushes had been used in China for centuries, until Addis's toothbrush most people in Britain cleaned their teeth by chewing sticks or using rags with an abrasive such as salt or soot. Addis was a ragmerchant from London's East End and his eureka moment is said to have come while he was imprisoned for rioting: the story goes that his first prototype toothbrush was made using a bone saved from one of his prison meals, with the design inspired by a broom in the corner of his cell. He began production on his release, and the new toothbrushes were an instant success, aided by the century's dramatic rise in the consumption of sugar. The original handles were made from bone, with pig-hair bristles attached by local women in their homes as piecework. Addis's company, later renamed Wisdom, went on to lead the way with the switch to celluloid handles (with nylon bristles), which like so much else were replaced by fully synthetic plastics in the 1950s.

Today, few of my flotsam toothbrushes are of this simple design, which dominated for more than two centuries. Most of my modern finds are instead a bewildering variety of fat, ergonomically designed handles – with angled necks and moulded contours inlaid with coloured plastics and rubbery grips. Given such complex materials and designs, hardly any will ever be recycled, meaning most modern toothbrushes end up in the bin.

We are, of course, also offered more hi-tech alternatives, including an array of electric toothbrushes (the Braun Oral-B Triumph not only pulsates, rotates and oscillates but also wirelessly transmits a map of your mouth to a screen as it brushes). Another recent innovation is the increasingly popular disposable electric toothbrush, a cheap sealed unit with a battery that can't be replaced. Like so much else on the market today, it is designed to be unrepairable. So after several months of use, these too will be incinerated or buried as landfill.

And what then? There is a revealing scene in the BBC documentary *The Secret Life of Landfill*, as the two presenters sort through waste dug from the sealed environment of a disused 1980s landfill site. After thirty or forty years the contents are shockingly unchanged. They pull out synthetic clothes, plastic packaging and disposable nappies, all in more or less the same condition as when they went in. They then find a newspaper, peeling apart its sodden pages to find that even this is still legible (and dated 1986). It is deeply disturbing to realize just how much of what my own family threw out in the 1980s – not least all that new technology – will still be out there, just grassed over and hidden from sight, with none of its finite resources reused.

While plastic is often seen as the main problem today, it is just one example of our short-term thinking about the long-term impacts of this wasting of resources. Despite increased awareness of the costs of our energy-hungry consumption, there is little sign that we are changing our lifestyles. We go on buying more of everything, from toys and clothes – British women buy twice as many as they did a decade ago – to electrical gadgets. Over the past decade, planned obsolescence has reached new heights with our screens and technology, which need replacing with ever-greater frequency.

All of which means we are also creating vast mountains of e-waste. It is our fastest growing waste problem, rising at double the rate of plastic. Only 20 per cent of electrical goods are recycled, so after these too have piled up in our cupboards and attics, the majority end up in landfill or incinerators. As with so much else, because none of these products are designed to encourage reuse, recycling or the recovery of materials, we are again throwing away valuable and finite resources, including the rare-earth and precious metals in the motherboards and microchips.

Like plastic, a common answer to the growing problem of

e-waste disposal is export to developing countries, with our obsolete goods often leaving Britain in the same truck-sized shipping containers they arrived in. Despite European regulations, a string of waste brokers can mean little is known about final destinations. And where a country's recycling lacks regulation, poverty can drive people to risk their health and local environment in efforts to extract those materials of value. Plastic and wires are burned in the open, soldered circuit boards melted for the lead, and microchips bathed in acid to extract tiny amounts of gold. Journalists visiting these areas describe the sickly, noxious stench of melted plastic, waste dumped at roadsides and on farmland, and toxic residues leaching out to pollute local waterways.

By then, though, it is not our problem.

8

Whitsand Bay, South Cornwall

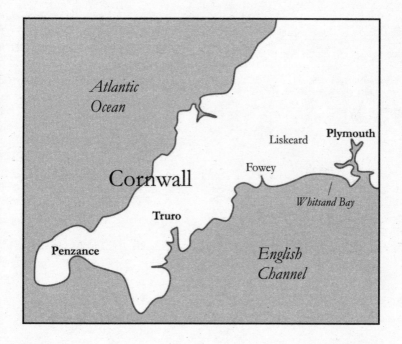

Atlantic Ocean

Cornwall

Liskeard

Plymouth

Fowey

Whitsand Bay

Truro

Penzance

English Channel

A few months later I left the car at the top of the cliffs at Whitsand Bay, a forty-minute drive along the coast from where I live. A path led down through otherwise impenetrable scrub and although at high tide there is hardly any beach, that morning the seabed sand stretched for miles. It had been windy again overnight and against the light, the sea had the texture of knifed oil paint.

I'd been visiting these coves regularly all winter, particularly after storms. It had been Britain's third year of naming storms and they'd begun with Storm Ophelia in October – ex-*hurricane* Ophelia, which arrived after those strikingly still days on the Isle of Sheppey. After that came Storm Brian, which, appropriately enough, brought my first plastic moustache – although by the winter's end I had three and a half.

As usual, it was the autumn storms that threw up the most seaweed, a clearing-out of the old summer growth, and as a result I'd spent those first visits poking through rotting heaps with a stick. Over the subsequent weeks and months, the weather and various scavengers had done their work and in time there was little but plastic at the top of the shore. Later storms had brought less weed but more plastic. This bay in particular tended to collect smaller pieces and many times that winter I'd walked out onto the sand to find it covered in swathes of tiny fragments.

Much of the debris there now had washed in a few weeks earlier with the latest storm, Emma. Yet it was only as I reached the bottom of the path that I saw plastic still carpeting much of the sand, graded in ever-smaller pieces as it ranged down the beach. Bright, multi-coloured lines meandered away across the sand, like those a child would make trailing a stick. They ended at the foot of the cliff, where more fragments floated on the surface of rockpools like a grim plastic soup. Like the plastic-filled North Sea fulmars, this was closer to home than the albatrosses and garbage patches, and a stark reminder of just how pervasive plastic has become in the marine environment, and consequently inside the creatures living there.

In the pools, much of the floating debris was nurdles. These are resin pellets about the size of lentils: the raw material that is melted to make almost all the plastic we buy, from carrier bags to plastic chairs. Never meant to be seen by consumers, the nurdles that turn up on beaches have been lost in industry spills during transport and manufacture. Being small and light, they are easily blown by the wind and wash down drains to enter our waterways. Eventually they end up in the oceans, where seabirds and fish mistake them for food. Today, like other microplastics, nurdles turn up on the most remote beaches and are found throughout the world's oceans.

I have a friend, Rob Arnold, who regularly cleans this beach, and several times during the winter I'd rounded the rocks to find him crouched over the strandline with a dustpan and brush. Originally an agricultural engineer, he has built an extraordinary machine that he wheels onto the beach; through a combination of sieves and flotation, it separates the nurdles and microplastics from seaweed and sand. The plastic is then bagged and removed, sometimes to Rob's house where he dries it on the front lawn and sorts it by hand. Following a beach-clean here the previous year, in an effort to raise awareness he'd decided to count the nurdles (by volume after the first cupful). This involved further separation stages using a series of graded mesh sieves – noisy in his quiet cul-de-sac – and then a hair dryer, inspired by the winnowing of grain. It turned out that from this one beach, in a single day, Rob and a group of local volunteers had removed 3.5 million nurdles.

The last time I'd bumped into him, I was with my daughter. Happily, she'd taken to beachcombing with renewed enthusiasm, inspired by the story of a shipment of Lego that was lost at sea. In 1997, the *Tokio Express*, a container ship bound for New York, was hit by a rogue wave twenty miles off Land's End. As the ship pitched steeply, sixty-two of its containers were lost overboard – one of which held almost 5 million pieces of Lego. Coincidentally, many were from sea-themed sets, including scuba tanks, life jackets, seaweed, divers' flippers, life rafts and octopuses. More than two decades later, pieces still regularly wash ashore in Cornwall, and finding them has become something of a cult hobby here. Of all the pieces recovered from the spill, best known are the 33,941 Lego dragons, and it was these that first sparked the interest of my dragon-hunter daughter (I found one recently while she was at school, and she took it badly).

So when we met Rob that day on the beach, she'd first compared Lego flippers, holding hers out proudly, before he began telling her about the rare pink nurdle. Amongst the 3.5 million nurdles collected that day on the beach clean, he'd found only one that was pink. The word *rare* worked its usual childhood magic and, although she's claimed to dislike pink since the age of five, she went on to spend every subsequent beach trip searching for an elusive pink nurdle. Recently, this culminated in the two of us scrabbling about on the floor of the downstairs toilet searching for the one she'd found and promptly lost. The boxes and jars that hold her finds now spill out from under her bed. So on occasions when I do need to pick my way across her bedroom, I vacillate between irritation at the mess and satisfaction that any scavenging gene has passed safely on.

Today, the debris on the beach was so small I had to crouch amongst it wearing reading glasses – beginning, methodically as usual, at the far end. Unlike the nurdles, most of it was no longer identifiable. Over the years, I'd gradually come to recognize the increasingly worn and fragmented stages in the breakdown of certain objects, usually those that turn up over and over again. Early finds that day included the end of a hair-curler pin, the coloured rings from the mouths of balloons and several shards from the lids of old Smarties tubes. (The lettered plastic lids are popular with beachcombers as they were discontinued in 2005; although most prized of all are the larger 'imperial' lids, dating from the 1950s to the 1970s, as the size of British Smarties tubes changed around the time of the shift from imperial to metric.)

By the time I'd made it halfway across the cove, I'd also found several of the green knobs from the stems of memorial poppies. These are common beach finds and I'd already bagged a couple of the poppies' black button middles. I'd learned from Rob that these too can be dated, to some extent, as those from modern poppies are printed with the words 'Poppy Appeal'. Today's said 'Haig Fund', meaning they were made before 1994. The earliest poppies – they have been sold since 1921 – were made from cloth with wire stems, held together by metal and later bitumen buttons. By 1967, though, this had all been replaced by plastic – meaning my 'Haig Fund' middles were between twenty-five and fifty years old.

After an hour or so of careful searching, my finds included a party popper with the distinctive bite-marks of fish, a hollow horse with holes in its sides – like those from 1970s bags of cowboys and Indians – and a black plastic Halloween fingernail, which looked comparatively recent. I also had two faded Pop-it beads: something of a craze in the 1950s and 1960s, they clicked together to form a necklace like a string of plastic pearls. (When I showed one to my mum recently, she made an excellent sound of recognition.)

The best find, though, was a green Monopoly house. I had six others at home – along with a single red hotel – and it was noticing small differences between them that got me wondering about the history of the board game. Lining them up on the kitchen table, I'd found that not only were they different shades of green (even allowing for fading at sea), but some were bungalows, some had overhanging roofs and four had no chimney. Of course, it turned out there were collectors who already knew a detailed history: the familiar London Monopoly board first sold in 1936, with its little green houses made of wood. In 1938 a special edition featured Bakelite houses, although most remained wooden into the 1950s. By the 1960s they were made from plastic, by the 1970s they had overhanging roofs and by the 1980s a chimney. Inevitably, I spent some time arranging my flotsam houses into order of age – before returning to the computer to discover a recent edition that brought it all up to date. The new version was Monopoly Empire. Instead of houses, players collect brand billboards (Nerf, Levis, Transformers, Virgin, etc) to fill a plastic tower, and its gold plastic tokens include a Coca-Cola bottle, a box of McDonald's fries and an Xbox 360 controller.

I made my way steadily down the shore through the drifts of microplastics, ever more reliant on my reading glasses as the finds became smaller. By the third cove I also had half an arm from a tiny baby, two plastic leaves and a toy soldier's knee. From the thousands of nondescript shards, I'd also chosen a few in bright Vanish pink, just in case.

Many pieces though were so small I could barely see them. At sea, plastic is embrittled by sunlight and fragmented by the action of waves, and there was no way to tell what these flecks once were. For centuries, perhaps millennia, they would simply go on breaking down into ever-smaller pieces. Today, many scientists believe that plastic will never completely disappear (we now know that nanoplastics – less than a billionth of a centimetre wide – can penetrate both the brain and embryo walls of fish). It is also now apparent that in the marine environment plastic is not the inert material it was once considered to be. The damage caused to wildlife is often pernicious, far less visible than entanglement or seabirds starving to death on full stomachs. Part of the problem is the additives: the flame-retardants, dyes and fungicides, the chemicals added to make the plastic harder or more flexible, more absorbent or waterproof, stronger or glossier. These additives are often untested and as the plastic breaks down they leach out into the water, or into the tissues of the creature it was eaten by. Once released into the body, some of these chemicals can affect hormone levels, development and behaviour, as well as disrupt immune systems and cause infertility. Phthalates, for example – additives used to soften everything from PVC shower curtains and food packaging to children's toys – do this through feminizing males.

Marine plastics also act as a sink, attracting free-floating chemical toxins that adhere to the surface in concentrations that can be a million times greater than in surrounding seawater. As well as the persistent, banned pollutants that linger in our oceans, these range from pesticides and fertilizers to the medicines and cleaning products washed down our drains, many of which have also been shown to affect marine creatures' immunity, fertility and development. And as the plastic continues to break down, it exposes more surface area, which in turn attracts more toxins.

The fragmentation also means that ever-smaller creatures can ingest the particles. I headed out around a rocky outcrop to get to the next cove and here blue mussels clustered together on the rocks. Like so many other marine creatures, from krill to blue whales, these mussels are filter feeders. As the tide returns, their shells open just enough to siphon water in through the gills, straining out any suspended particles of food. In this way, a single mussel can filter up to twenty litres of seawater a day, leaving them vulnerable to ingesting microplastics drifting in the water. One British study found that 60 per cent of the mussels tested contained microplastics, and in parts of the south-east this was as high as 80 per cent. (When other debris such as cotton and rayon was included, it rose to 100 per cent.) To date, wherever scientists have looked, the mussel population has contained plastic, even in the seemingly pristine waters of the Arctic.

There is now also plenty of evidence that plastic is ingested at the very base of the marine food chain. Some of the most striking images I've seen were taken by plankton scientist Dr Richard Kirby, based in Plymouth a few miles away along the coast. Beneath his microscope, single drops of local seawater become luminous otherworlds, teeming with the glassy outlines of plankton. In recent years, many of his filmed samples have also contained microplastics. In one, plankton is trapped in a tangle of synthetic microfibres; in another a mess of fibres are caught in the fine, sticky tentacles of a comb jelly – the strands perhaps from synthetic clothing, degraded fishing rope or flushed wet wipes. A third shows a single fibre ingested by a microscopic arrow worm. Inside its lifeless, transparent body, the fibre is clearly visible: a single dark thread looping around to entirely block the passage of food through its gut.

As plankton forms a large part of the diet of many fish and other marine creatures, this is another way that plastic and its toxins move up the food chain. Another Plymouth study showed a third of UK-caught fish now contain plastic. The associated toxins also accumulate in the tissues of higher predators – seals, dolphins, whales, polar bears – where again they can interfere with organ function, growth and development. Disturbingly, these toxins can also be passed on through a mother's milk.

In the next cove I sat down to look through my finds. As on other visits that winter, they now included a couple of wheels from toy cars, several authentic-looking grey plastic 'pebbles' and a small handful of biro lids and ends. Again I recognized some from the ubiquitous Cristal Bic. As usual, though, I'd seen none of the familiar clear plastic tubes that form the body of the pen, despite the fact that in 2006 Bic celebrated production of its 100 billionth biro. The reason is that the tubes are made from solid polystyrene, which doesn't float. Instead – like more than half the plastic in our oceans – the denser tubes sink to the seafloor.

Ultimately, this is where much of the rest is headed, too, because as plastic continues to break down – into micro- and nano-sized particles – much of it eventually drifts to the seafloor. So inevitably, both plastic and the toxins it carries are now found inside the creatures living there. Findings range from microbeads extracted from crabs to the associated toxins causing harm to lugworms; a lobster caught off the coast of Canada even had the blue and white Pepsi logo somehow imprinted on a claw. In recent years, plastic has been found in marine creatures' stomachs, in their tissues and organs, and lodged inside their gills.

Synthetic fibres have even been found inside creatures living in the deepest parts of the world's oceans, including the Mariana Trench, almost seven miles beneath the surface. In one study, every single crustacean tested had man-made debris in its stomach or muscles, including nylon, polyvinyl and that most common of our single-use plastics, polyethylene. While the Thames might no longer be the reeking 'Stygian pool' of the nineteenth century, our plastic waste and its associated toxins are now found throughout the world's rivers and oceans.

In the 2013 documentary *A Plastic Ocean*, images shot from a deep-sea submersible show the seabed a mile and a half beneath the surface of the Mediterranean. In those dark, still waters, the sub's lights slip over an eerie moonscape softened by what scientists call 'marine snow'. Minute flecks drift down through the water, coming to settle on the seafloor as they have done for hundreds of millions of years. Except that now, along with the usual sediment and organic remains, they include microscopic fragments of synthetic plastics. As ever, in those remote snowy drifts, it is the shapes of familiar objects that shock: the plastic drinks bottle, the yoghurt pot and carrier bag, the disposable cup. On the still, cold floor of the abyss, in perpetual darkness, our waste is going nowhere and will simply accumulate.

The sub's images of drifting sediment remind me of fossils. In much the same way, the remains of those extinct creatures came to rest on the floor of ancient seas and estuaries, and were buried beneath the weight of later sediment. Gradually, as minerals percolated down, a perfect replica formed: of a vertebra, an ammonite or shark's tooth, or the tubes of ship-worm burrows I've often found on Sheppey. This last is a trace fossil. Unlike true fossils, which are the fossilized remains of living organisms, trace fossils are impressions those creatures left behind. And these impressions – burrows or borings; perhaps footprints or teeth marks – provide rich clues as to how a long-extinct species lived and behaved.

So I wonder about the sunken biro tubes, about the wheel-less cars and plastic drinks bottles lying out there on the ocean floor with all the rest of our waste. In tens of millions of years, a tiny fraction will survive as trace fossils – sometimes referred to as technofossils. As many of our old dumps and landfill sites are on coasts and low-lying estuaries, they will be amongst the first places lost to rising seas. So they'll be the first to be buried in sediment. To a future palaeontologist, trying to piece together the distant past from traces in a band of rock, what will those technofossils say of how we lived?

Today, our lives are driven by ever-quicker obsolescence. Our stuff – from washing machines and sofas to smartphones and under-used kitchen gadgets – is now cheaper to replace than to repair. These products have revolutionized our lives and made everything easier. Yet this has only been possible because their true costs are not reflected in their price tags.

With so much produced overseas, it is easy for those material and environmental burdens to remain out of sight (while imported goods are produced for us, for example, their associated carbon emissions don't appear in our national statistics). As if conjured from nothing, these products cross oceans to reach us, pass briefly through our lives and then are whisked away into the waste stream. With so much of this one-way journey hidden from view, it has been easy for the raw materials to lose their value. In turn, as if these precious resources were limitless, we've felt increasingly free to waste them.

All these things – our wastefulness and over-consumption, our continued dependence on fossil fuels, our use of cheap, disposable plastics – are tightly bound together. Today, with almost all plastic made from the by-products of fossil-fuel extraction, the same corporations, such as Shell and Exxon Mobil, are involved in the production of both petrochemicals and the raw plastic resins. (In the US, the current fracking boom has brought cheaper resins and a sharp rise in investment in new plastic production facilities, which will simply drive future growth.)

As it's turned out, there were of course limits after all; it's just taken us a while to see the true costs and ramifications of our consumption. Of them all, the most difficult to face has been climate change. We have known for decades now that our reliance on fossil fuels is affecting earth's climate. As far back as the 1990s, policymakers began adopting a boundary level for 'dangerous' climate change of 2 °C above preindustrial temperatures. At the time of writing we are already above 1 °C. Today, that 2 °C threshold is widely seen as a tipping point, beyond which any further rise will trigger dangerous feedback loops. Above it, there is less Arctic ice to reflect the sun's heat, and natural carbon sinks like permafrost will start releasing large amounts of stored CO_2. Climate models show this leading to runaway warming, which would be irreversible.

Despite the politicization of climate change and subsequent confusion around the science, the first decade of this century did see a sharp rise in public awareness. Increasingly, people came to accept its causes and effects, and the need to move away from fossil fuels to renewable sources of energy. But with the financial crisis of 2008 this faded from the media, giving the impression that the issue had lost its urgency. Since then, our efforts towards emissions reduction have been modest, and many targets are likely to be missed. While I've been writing, the United States has pledged to withdraw from the Paris Agreement, signed in 2016, which has the aim of keeping the global temperature rise below 2 °C by the end of the century.

But rather than weaning ourselves off oil, coal and gas – and leaving carbon safely in the ground – we have instead pushed ahead with new, often riskier and dirtier methods of extraction, ranging from fracking and the mining of tar sands to deep-water and Arctic drilling; as climate change causes glaciers to recede, this is simply revealing new areas for exploration.

Climate scientists now believe it is 'extremely unlikely' that by 2100 we will have stayed within that 2 °C threshold. Recent models suggest it is more likely to be above 3 °C, with feedback loops locking us in to a rise of 4 °C.

As with a 2 °C rise, 4 °C doesn't sound like much – particularly for those of us living at northern latitudes. Yet the reality would be very different. With a rise of 4 °C, melting ice sheets and thermal expansion would cause a rise in sea level of many metres, meaning inundation of major world cities. Across the globe there would be a dramatic increase in extreme weather events such as destructive storms and surges, droughts, hurricanes and heatwaves. Desertification and water scarcity would increase dramatically. Entire ecosystems and an estimated one-sixth of all species would be lost. (Since the 1970s, human activity has already wiped out 60 per cent of the world's mammals, birds, fish and reptiles.) We would also lose vast tracts of cultivable farmland. While some parts of the world would be worse affected than others – often developing countries with the least responsibility for climate change – the effects of such reduced resources would be global. Many millions of displaced refugees would stress populations everywhere, widening divisions and provoking massive social unrest. As the World Bank puts it, 'There is no certainty that adaptation to a 4 °C world is possible.' In his 2015 book *Don't Even Think About It: Why Our Brains Are Wired to Ignore Climate Change*, George Marshall describes climate scientists using the phrase 'four degrees' as shorthand for environmental, social and economic collapse.

There is now no doubt that earth's temperature *will* rise by 4 °C; all that is uncertain is how long it will take. New data and modelling techniques mean scientists' projections are constantly shifting – usually moving the date closer – and every year their warnings become clearer and more stark. With rapid world population growth and our high-energy, high-consumption lifestyles increasingly exported around the globe, we cannot go on as we are. Without deep cuts in our emissions, some recent models predict a 4 °C rise by the end of this century, or even before. Which brings it within the lifetime of my own children.

So how do we possibly manage to ignore it? Reading the science is deeply disturbing. Like most people, across the political spectrum, I'd managed to be aware of the issues but stay vague on details. Along with its politicization, climate change is also a complex and unprecedented threat with so many unknowns and a solution that requires the cooperation of vast numbers of people across the world. In behavioural studies, it is notoriously difficult to get groups of strangers to cooperate, especially around the use of shared resources. Fifty years ago, taking cattle grazing in nineteenth-century Britain as an example, the ecologist Garrett Hardin described this phenomenon as the 'tragedy of the commons'. For on seeing others take more for themselves, our usual response is to do the same, even if this means that eventually we all lose.

As well as feeling powerless, most of us also struggle to accept responsibility ourselves – which involves the thorny questioning of our own values and way of life; there is also the social pressure to conform to norms around us, with high-consumption lifestyles now so much a part of our identity. To date, we have therefore been far more comfortable viewing climate change as a problem for future generations. In doing so, we avoid the need for any immediate action that might override our short-term interests – which is just as true of the politicians we elect.

Our most common response has been to look away. If climate change does come up, it is easier to avoid it: change channel, skim the article, swipe past the link. We pay brief attention and move on, because most of us prefer not to know the details. We play down the threat so it feels more distant, imagining some technological solution will come along to save us. We are also adept at finding ways to diminish our own responsibility – justifying our own wasteful or energy-hungry choices and magnifying the benefits of positive actions (as if the feel-good factor of recycling absolves us from responsibility in other areas such as travel).

All of which leaves us free to carry on as usual, creating what is sometimes described as a massive global 'bystander effect', in which everyone waits to see what others will do before they act. Through the decades of debate – over whether or not climate change was happening at all, and if man-made emissions were actually responsible – we have lost so much time. In the 1990s climate change was considered a problem for our great-grandchildren; now it is one that will affect our own children. As the scientists continue to tell us, in putting off meaningful action to address our wastefulness and addiction to fossil fuels, we have lost the option of incremental change. Without sweeping changes now, our children will have uncontrollable change forced upon them.

Our reaction cannot be to simply throw up our hands in despair at the scale of the problem. We do need to make changes within our own lives, from giving up some level of convenience and flying less to avoiding unnecessary packaging and single-use products. But, most importantly, we need systemic change.

Solutions to these complex, urgent and deeply connected crises require the same degree of creativity and ingenuity that got us here in the first place, from the innovations of the Industrial Revolution to the sophisticated psychology that persuades us to buy. Crucially, we need to drastically reduce our emissions and switch to renewable sources of energy, leaving carbon in the ground. We also need to rethink the whole way we design and manufacture goods, taking into account a product's entire lifecycle so resources are valued and waste is minimized. When goods are designed for reuse, repair, recycling or remanufacture, the materials are then recovered or kept in use, rather than ending up in landfill, incinerators or our oceans. In ensuring this happens, we move away from the current one-way system, sometimes described as 'take, make, waste', to one that is circular and so closer to systems found in nature. A way of encouraging this is 'extended producer responsibility', whereby manufacturers become responsible – either physically or financially – for recycling, reuse or buy-back schemes (particularly appropriate for e-waste, with its heavy toxic burden). By designing waste out of the system, resources are kept in use for as long as possible, allowing us to extract the maximum value from them.

For change on the scale that's needed, though, we have to put pressure on businesses and government through protest and our vote. Because change will only happen once they know enough people see the need for it now – and not at some comfortably distant point in the future.

I rounded more rocks with my bags full of plastic, the contents so different to the river finds I'd hauled back from previous centuries. It had been oddly appropriate to see the Thames finds gradually accumulate in the house that past year, only to be swamped by plastic over winter. For in following a trail of our waste and its effects over generations, I'd found it increasingly disturbing to realize that such vast change had taken place in so short a space of time. How astonished my grandad would be at the contents of our bins today – and those earlier generations even more so. For until the boom years of the 1950s, the things we discarded had remained more or less unchanged for millennia: broken pottery and glass, ash from fires, food waste such as bones and shells. These were simple materials that in time would break down and return to the earth. Yet today the products that flow through our lives are often so complex that the materials they are made from will never be recovered for reuse. Over the course of a single lifetime – my mum's – we have become a truly throwaway culture, recklessly squandering our planet's resources.

The next cove, I could already see, was full of plastic. I stopped, suddenly sick of it all. This was a feeling I'd had before on this beach, often about this far along. There was just too much of it – too much to bear looking through any more. So I turned away, and headed out to meet the incoming tide.

The previous weekend, I'd sat at our kitchen table drinking tea with my mum. After looking at a few new things in the cabinet of finds, we'd begun talking about the recent shift in attitudes towards disposable plastic. This was part of what the media had dubbed the 'Blue Planet Effect', following the programme's final, powerful episode with its focus on the effects man has had on the oceans. Over subsequent months, this had prompted a variety of campaigns, from deposit-return schemes for plastic bottles to bans on cotton buds and plastic straws (I'd seen plenty of all three on beaches that winter). In the communities around where I live, local people and businesses had also come together to discuss ways of reducing their reliance on disposable plastics. And I'd found the subject cropping up in chance conversations, with people who'd never mentioned it before. At the time, it was a glimpse of something I hadn't properly considered. Seeing those around us care enough to make changes themselves is a powerful motivator; a sense of mutual support and shared, multiplied efforts can move us on from feeling we're too isolated and powerless to have any effect. By the year's end, it would culminate in 'single-use' being announced as the *Collins Dictionary* Word of the Year, as it encompassed 'a global movement to kick our addiction to disposable products'.

It felt like a significant shift. Through the prism of my own heightened awareness, I hoped it might also be the trigger that prompted wider concerns around the urgency of our need to face up to climate change. Since I'd begun writing the book, this was something that had happened repeatedly. I'd jolt awake to the radio at 6 a.m., to a headline about a new report on melting icecaps, or a stark warning from scientists of how little time we had left to make the necessary changes. And I'd think, this is it. This is the piece of information that will get everyone's attention. Yet time and again it wasn't the case, for, as NASA scientist Kate Marvel says, 'When we talk about climate change, we sometimes assume people will be swayed by one more graph, one more coherent argument. But that's not how people work. More facts don't change minds, and deeply held views don't always dictate behaviour.'

At the kitchen table, I began speaking about this to my mum. I described how over the past year I'd struggled with the overwhelming scale of the issues, how I'd swung between pessimism, frustration and hope – and at times despair. I then slipped into talking about the magnitude of the consequences of failing to act. I'd been speaking for a while when she looked away abruptly and let out a long breath: weary, dismayed and uncomfortable.

'I'm glad I . . .' she said, but tailed off.

She wasn't able to say it. It was too big, too unsettling, and a space hung in the air between us. I thought I knew what it was. At seventy-five, she was relieved that, for her generation, this wasn't their problem.

My daughter, now at secondary school, passed through the kitchen then, distracted and looking for food. Climate change was something they'd learned about in primary school, in clear, uncomplicated terms. A few years earlier she'd come home and described what they'd learned that day, and listened carefully as I agreed wholeheartedly.

'Then why do we drive a car that needs petrol?'

I'd begun to answer. I no longer recall what I said, just that I too tailed off as I became aware of how hollow my justifications sounded.

Far more aware than we ever were, her generation has known of the consequences of our wastefulness from the start. So it is tempting to see that this is where the hope lies, that they will have the understanding and motivation to make the necessary changes. But we are running out of time. They have also been born at this pinnacle of ease and convenience. All they've known is a world of endless growth, where everything is just a click away, where stuff travels from distant continents on ghostly container ships and flows into our lives through unseen 'fulfilment' centres – to be whisked away by the binmen and not thought of again.

At Whitsand Bay the tide comes in with deceptive speed, surging in over near-flat sand, and in the end I hurry back through the shallows, scrambling over rocks to reach the cove I started out from. All the miles of open sand have gone.

I stay on for another half-hour, sitting watching as the waves reach the lowest of the strandlines. The first do no more than push the microplastics a little further up the beach. Yet in what seems no time at all the waves are surging on past, re-floating it all in a plastic soup. I stand up with my bags of rubbish. Swept up in this last century's rush of consumption, we have disregarded the crucial implication of the word *consumption* itself – the using up of finite resources.

Acknowledgements

I am deeply grateful to Mark Richards, a wonderful editor and publisher, for time and space as the book found its course, and for clarity in the murk of early drafts. I would also like to thank Abigail Scruby and Will Atkins for fine editing and copy-editing, Tracy Watts for drawing such good maps, Sara Marafini for a wonderful cover and Caroline Westmore and the rest of the team at John Murray.

As a work-in-progress, nine months in, the book received the Royal Society of Literature Giles St Aubyn Award for Non-Fiction, which has been a wonderful support in so many ways (not least the under-desk heater it paid for that winter). I would like to thank everyone involved, including staff at the Royal Society of Literature, the judges and the St Aubyn family, in particular Fiona St Aubyn for her warm and generous enthusiasm for the book. It was also how I met fellow awardee Jo Jolly, whose subsequent friendship, support and encouragement have been invaluable.

I am particularly grateful to friends who read through drafts and chapters, and gave their thoughts and much-needed encouragement: Rob Arnold, Pamela Dearing, Richard Cowen, Tessa Jackson, Sue Lord, Amelia Wise, Claire Wallerstein, Sue Harmes, Mandy Walker and my mum.

For generosity with their time and knowledge I would like to thank Stuart Wyatt, Finds Liaison Officer at the Museum of London, Roger Betts, Keith Robinson, Tracey Williams,

Malcolm Russell, Monika Buttling-Smith, Dave Atkin, Lena Crowder at the Minster Gatehouse Museum and Chris Knight.

I would also like to thank fellow beachcombers and friends Laurie Harpum, Jo Atherton, Sarah McCartney, Lois Wakeman, Lynda White and Ronnie Creswell. For generous shore-found gifts and swaps I am grateful to Tricia Scott for the sea-worn mangle roller, Anna Pidcock for the golf ball and kelp, Tracey Williams for the sea fan with washing instructions and Lynne Graves for a bent teaspoon. Along the way, I've also learned a great deal from various online and real-life communities of beachcombers, beach cleaners and mudlarks, and have appreciated the often wonderfully niche knowledge they've been happy to share.

I am grateful to my mum, dad and brother, for all the stories, and for more than I could possibly begin to say here. I would also like to thank Eddy Tolladay and Sylvie Mellish for sharing their memories, and both Sylvie and her late husband Peter for a love of books and libraries passed on through my mum.

Most of all I would like to thank Saan, Joe and Erin, for love, for not minding when the house was overtaken by the 'beach detritus', and for the inspiration of their curiosity.

Further Reading

Ackroyd, Peter, *London: The Biography* (Vintage, 2001)

——, *Thames: Sacred River* (Vintage, 2008)

Ashton, Rosemary, *One Hot Summer: Dickens, Darwin, Disraeli and the Great Stink of 1858* (Yale University Press, 2018)

Ayre, Julian, and Wroe-Brown, Robin, *The London Millennium Bridge: Excavation of the Medieval and Later Waterfronts at Peter's Hill, City of London, and Bankside, Southwark* (Museum of London Archaeology, 2002)

Barton, Nicholas, *The Lost Rivers of London: A Study of Their Effects Upon London and Londoners, and the Effects of London and Londoners on Them* (Historical Publications, 1992)

Bunker, Francis, *Seaweeds of Britain and Ireland* (Wild Nature Press, 2017)

Carson, Rachel, *The Sea Around Us* trilogy (Unicorn Press, 2014; orig. 1941, 1950, 1955)

——, *The Edge of the Sea* (Unicorn Press, 2015; orig. 1955)

Cohen, Nathalie, and Wragg, Elliott, *The River's Tale: Archaeology on the Thames Foreshore in Greater London* (Museum of London Archaeology, 2017)

Conrad, Joseph, *The Mirror of the Sea* (Nature Classics Library, 2013; orig. 1906)

Dee, Tim, *Landfill* (Little Toller Books, 2018)

Diamond, Jared, *Guns, Germs and Steel: A Short History of Everybody For the Last 13,000 Years* (Vintage, 1998)

Dickens, Charles, *Our Mutual Friend* (Penguin, 1997; orig. 1865)

——, *Dickens's Dictionary of London*, 1879

Ebbesmeyer, Curtis, and Scigliano, Eric, *Flotsametrics and the Floating*

World: How One Man's Obsession with Runaway Sneakers and Rubber Ducks Revolutionized Ocean Science (Harper Perennial, 2010)

Fletcher, Edward, *Bottle Collecting* (Blandford Press, 1972)

Fort, Tom, *The Book of Eels: On the Trail of the Thin-Heads* (HarperCollins, 2003)

Freinkel, Susan, *Plastic: A Toxic Love Story* (Houghton Mifflin Harcourt, 2011)

George, Rose, *Deep Sea and Foreign Going: Inside Shipping, the Invisible Industry that Brings You 90% of Everything* (Portobello Books, 2014)

Girling, Richard, *Rubbish! Dirt on Our Hands and Crisis Ahead* (Eden Project, 2005)

——, *Sea Change: Britain's Coastal Catastrophe* (Eden Project, 2012)

Grose, Francis, *1811 Dictionary of the Vulgar Tongue* (CreateSpace, 2012)

Hoare, Philip, *The Sea Inside* (Fourth Estate, 2014)

Hone, Donovan, *Moby-Duck: The True Story of 28,800 Bath Toys Lost at Sea* (Union Books, 2012)

Hounsell, Peter, *London's Rubbish: Two Centuries of Dirt, Dust and Disease in the Metropolis* (Amberley, 2013)

Jackson, Lee, *Dirty Old London: The Victorian Fight Against Filth* (Yale University Press, 2015)

Johnson, Steven, *The Ghost Map: A Street, an Epidemic and the Hidden Power of Urban Networks* (Penguin, 2008)

Klein, Naomi, *This Changes Everything: Capitalism vs. the Climate* (Penguin, 2015)

——, *On Fire: The Burning Case for a New Green Deal* (Allen Lane, 2019)

Kolbert, Elizabeth, *Field Notes from a Catastrophe: Man, Nature, and Climate Change* (Bloomsbury USA, 2015)

——, *The Sixth Extinction: An Unnatural History* (Bloomsbury, 2015)

Leonard, Annie, *The Story of Stuff: The Impact of Overconsumption on the Planet, Our Communities and Our Health – And How We Can Make It Better* (Simon & Schuster, 2011)

Lewis, Simon, and Maslin, Mark A., *The Human Planet: How We Created the Anthropocene* (Pelican, 2018)

Licence, Tom, *What the Victorians Threw Away* (Oxbow Books, 2015)

Lichtenstein, Rachel, *Estuary: Out from London to the Sea* (Penguin, 2017)

Maiklem, Lara, *Mudlarking: Lost and Found on the River Thames* (Bloomsbury, 2019)

Marshall, George, *Don't Even Think About It: Why Our Brains Are Wired to Ignore Climate Change* (Bloomsbury USA, 2015)

Mayhew, Henry, *London Labour and the London Poor* (Wordsworth Classics, 2008; orig. 1851)

Minter, Adam, *Junkyard Planet: Travels in the Billion-Dollar Trash Trade* (Bloomsbury, 2014)

Monbiot, George, *Heat: How We Can Stop the Planet Burning* (Penguin, 2007)

Moore, Charles, *Plastic Ocean: How a Sea Captain's Chance Discovery Launched a Determined Quest to Save the Oceans* (Avery Publishing, 2012)

Morris, Ian, *Why the West Rules – For Now: The Patterns of History and What They Reveal About the Future* (Profile, 2011)

Nagle, Robin, *Picking Up: On the Streets and Behind the Trucks with the Sanitation Workers of New York City* (Farrar, Straus & Giroux, 2014)

Nicolson, Adam, *The Seabird's Cry: The Lives and Loves of Puffins, Gannets and Other Ocean Voyagers* (William Collins, 2018)

Noel Hume, Ivor, *Treasure in the Thames* (Muller, 1956)

Parker, Matthew, *The Sugar Barons: Family, Corruption, Empire and War* (Windmill Books, 2012)

Rathje, William, and Murphy, Cullen, *Rubbish! The Archaeology of Garbage* (HarperCollins Australia, 1992)

Roberts, Callum, *Ocean of Life: The Fate of Man and the Sea* (Penguin, 2013)

Rogers, Heather, *Gone Tomorrow: The Hidden Life of Garbage* (New Press, 2005)

Sandling, Ted, *London in Fragments: A Mudlark's Treasures* (Frances Lincoln, 2016)

Slade, Giles, *Made to Break: Technology and Obsolescence in America* (Harvard University Press, 2007)

Sprackland, Jean, *Strands: A Year of Discoveries on the Beach* (Vintage, 2013)

Stevens, Pauline, *Lower Halstow: The Story of a Village in Kent* (Pauline Stevens, 1999)

Strasser, Susan, *Waste and Want: A Social History of Trash* (Holt McDougal, 2000)

Talling, Paul, *London's Lost Rivers* (Random House, 2011)

Trentmann, Frank, *Empire of Things: How We Became a World of Consumers, from the Fifteenth Century to the Twenty-First* (Penguin, 2016)

Trewhella, Steve, and Hatcher, Julie, *The Essential Guide to Beachcombing and the Strandline* (Wild Nature Press, 2015)

Vance, Gaia, *Adventures in the Anthropocene: A Journey to the Heart of the Planet We Made* (Vintage, 2016)

Wallace-Wells, David, *The Uninhabitable Earth: A Story of the Future* (Penguin, 2019)

Wilde, Oscar, *The Picture of Dorian Gray* (Penguin, 2003; orig. 1891)

Note on the Cover

While writing *Rag and Bone*, my collection of shore finds spread to fill boxes, drawers and kitchen cupboards. Some are stored in old printsetters' trays, as shown on the front and back covers of this book.

Front cover includes:

Action Man 'hard hand' (1966–1973)
Pewter blow-hole button (1650–1700)
Bone comb (1600s–1700s)
Cycle reflector (came free with Kellogg's Cornflakes in 1989)
Bone toothbrush (c. 1800s)
Plastic roll-on deodorant ball (2000s)
Lead toothpaste tubes (1800s–1900s)
Plastic wedding cake dove (1970s–2000s)
'Ring type' thimble (1450–1600)
Marlboro Man lighter (1970s–1990s)
Lego dragon (lost at sea in 1997)
Lead knight and horse's head (c. 1800s)
Turtle Wax car air freshener (1980s)
Disposable plastic razor and ice cream spoon (1970s–2000s)
Codd marbles (c. 1800s)
Plastic cherub, dinosaurs, goat and kangaroo (1970s–2000s)
Hand-made pins (1400s–1700s)

Fragment of a Delftware 'scroll salt' (c. 1600s)
Ceramic doll parts (c. 1800s)
Light bulb fittings (c. 1900s)
Plastic army men (1970s–2000s)
Brass toggle light switch (c. 1900s)
Death's head button moulds (c. 1700s)

Back cover includes:

Jug handle, Surrey whiteware (1350–1400s)
Buttons: bone, metal, mother-of-pearl and plastic (1700s–2000s)
'Drain hole' from a sugar cone mould (1600s–1700s)
Lead trade token with anchor design (1787–1790s)
Plastic soy sauce fish from takeaway sushi (2000s)
Crotal bell (1600s–1700s)
Clay pipe bowls and stems (1600s–1800s)
Glass bottle stoppers (c. 1800s)
Waste from making bone buttons or beads by hand (pre 1900s)
Plastic toothbrush with copper wire (1900s)
Hand-made nails (c. 1500s–1700s)
Coral and a money cowrie (likely from ballast dumped c. 1700s)
Combed slipware (1690–1830)
Bone combs (c. 1600s–1700s)
Green 'poison bottle' (1800s–1900s)
Iron musket ball (1800s)

Index